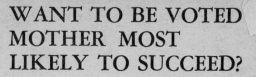

WANT TO BE VOTED MOTHER MOST LIKELY TO SUCCEED?

It's easy. When Junior starts singing the "What Shall I Do Now?" blues, set him to work making:

Puppets out of paper bags

Cabin Cruisers out of milk cartons

Snowballs out of soap and water

Ingenious? Wait till you see how easy they are! And how delighted your child is with his own handiwork.

The instructions are all here in this bright, imaginative book by a famous TV personality who's a wizard at keeping kids busy. Each page is crammed with ideas for vacation and party fun, rainy-day games and sick-in-bed times, for children of all ages. And the only materials needed are simple household supplies.

With this incredible book, you face only one problem: Who gets first crack at it after the kids are in bed—you or Dad?

It's that fascinating!

". . . a 'must' for the parents of the young set. . . . a most attractively done book . . . a lifesaver for mothers and their offspring."

Marblehead *Town Crier*

HERE'S WHAT THE CRITICS SAID:

"Mothers . . . will give all-out praise to FUN WITH THE KIDS."

Albuquerque (N. M.) *Tribune*

". . . a complete fun-book for families of all sizes and ages."

Jackson *Sun*

". . . one of the most resourceful books about how to keep children amused and out of trouble . . ."

London (Ont.) *Free Press*

"This wonderful book will give aid and comfort to parents and teachers . . ."

Bangor (Me.) *News*

"A lot of ideas, colorfully presented, for year-around enjoyment over a wide age range."

Windsor (Ont.) *Star*

". . . will be a joy to parents . . ."

Rochester *Democrat & Chronicle*

KISSES
10¢

FUN
WITH THE
KIDS

SHARI LEWIS

Drawings by Larry Lurin
Photographs by Chano

MB

A Macfadden-Bartell Book

THIS BOOK IS THE COMPLETE TEXT
OF THE HARDCOVER EDITION

✳

TO MY MOTHER AND FATHER,
who have been the source of
so much fun for so many, many
children

✳

A MACFADDEN BOOK....1964

MACFADDEN BOOKS are published by
Macfadden-Bartell Corporation
205 East 42nd Street, New York, New York, 10017

Library of Congress Catalog Card Number: 60-15183

The photographs on pages 69, 70, and 71 are from the
Cleanliness Bureau, New York

CONTENTS

Fun with the Kids

Acknowledgments

I've been "doing it myself" in the play field ever since I can remember, and through the years, many people have contributed ideas and suggestions for my television "home-play" shows. I am grateful to them all, and my only regret is that in acknowledging some donors, I will be omitting other inventive individuals and research organizations who have helped me often and well.

Nevertheless, I must thank the outstanding women - - - - - - at Brown and Roland, which handles creative concepts and uses for both Minnesota Mining and Manufacturing Company's Scotch tape and Q-Tip cotton swabs, made by Q-Tips, Inc.

at The Cleanliness Bureau of the Association of American Soap and Glycerine Producers, Inc.

at Binney and Smith, Inc., manufacturers of Crayola crayons and Artista paints.

I am also very thankful for the aid and advice afforded me by the Children's Creative Art Foundation (under the direction of Dr. H. Conant).

A few of the play activities in this text have appeared in *Good Housekeeping Magazine* (in the "Shari Lewis Small Fry Scrapbook"). *Good Housekeeping* has granted me permission to publish these items here, and I do appreciate their co-operation and enthusiasm.

The undergraduate students in recreational leadership at the Yeshiva University have devised and explored many play projects, and their experimentation has been of great interest and assistance.

From my editor at Doubleday, Elliott Schryver, I've received creative guidance every inch of the way.

I also want to thank Frank Lewis for the hours he has spent expediting the completion of this book.

But most of all, I am grateful to my husband, Jeremy Tarcher, for the good counsel and strong shoulder he offers me at all times.

Introduction

"Play with me, Daddy." That's a normal request, but if your youngster has passed the "patty-cake" stage, it may evoke any one of a number of other responses. You may ask yourself "Why must I play with my child—he ought to learn to entertain himself." Or perhaps you may wonder *"How* can I best have fun with my kids?"

The "why" is not a selfish question. It is indeed important that a child learn to be independent and self-reliant. In later life, most of his greatest creative accomplishments will develop as a result of solitary effort and thought. But children need grown-up guidance.

This book is not a compilation of sustained child-parent activities, but rather a suggestion of play paths along which you may direct your youngster. Play is a child's "work," and the best way to encourage good "work" habits is to provide adequate work area, proper materials, encouragement, and plenty of time.

Not every child is a gifted child, but every youngster has gifts and deserves the right to discover them. These gifts need not be of an artistic or intellectual nature, any more than the end product of the play (or "work") need be a tangible object. The gifts discovered and developed can be as simple (and as valuable) as concentration, or the appreciation of things of an artistic nature. Desirable ends of a play period might be the glow of accomplishment, a good working relationship with the parent or another child, or just the stimulating atmosphere around the house.

One researcher found that among successful artists and scientists, the most consistent characteristic is the ability to work hard and for long periods of time on a single problem. Now, no one can develop a sustained interest span by watching television or constantly coloring meaningless pre-drawn pictures in a coloring book.

These experts say that generations to come will have more leisure time. If your youngster is to enjoy this free time, he must be shown the way—otherwise there will be a world full of spectators, with almost no one worth watching!

It's important that this gentle but generous guidance be given at home as well as in school, for no one can truly find himself in a crowd. In developing your youngster's sense of security, nothing will contribute as much as sincere interest from you.

That is why I think we should play *with* our children. How can you best have fun with your kids? These pages are devoted to helping you to help your youngster to help himself!

CHAPTER I

Fun Indoors on a Rainy Day

There lives not a mother who has not heard the "What-Shall-I-Do-Now Cha-Cha-Cha." Most youngsters, in their sweet, singsong voices, start softly humming this familiar refrain on the morning of the first rainy day. After a week of dreary indoor play, they are loudly alternating this theme with another —the "I-Haven't-Got-Anything-to-Play-with Blues."

Here are some activity suggestions that will keep your children busy, safe, and relatively quiet for hours.

The best way to plan play for a rainy day is to see what materials you have available in your home. Here are a few household items, any or all of which will provide you with a day, a week, or even a month (should your community be monsoon prone) of contented rainy-day play.

Waxed milk and cream cartons	Pencils
Paper cups	Pennies
Paper plates	Poster paint
Straws	Empty cereal boxes
Toothpicks	Old clothes
Inexpensive plates	Sewing materials—thimble,
Pots and pans	needle, thread, scissors,
Soap: cake, liquid, flakes or	bits of fabric, buttons
detergent	Clothespins
Old towels	Old discarded playing cards
Kitchen funnels	Laundry shirt cardboards
Vegetable food coloring	Old magazines
Bits of foods—e.g., nuts,	Modeling clay
beans	Crayons
Aluminum foil	Paints
Paper grocery and cleaners'	Rubber cement or paste
bags	Cellophane tape
Cardboard grocery cartons	Balloons
	Rubber bands

Decide what projects or games you are going to play, gather all the necessary materials together, and find a place where the player (or players) won't be in the way of the house-cleaning activities—it's very difficult to concentrate on anything when you feel that at any moment you may be sucked up into the vacuum cleaner.

EASY TOYS

These are as much fun to play with as they are to make. All of them, and most of the other activities in this chapter, are for quiet play for one or more children.

JIGSAW PUZZLES

These can be as easy (for a four-year-old) or as complicated (for a twelve-year-old) as you like, so before you start cutting your jigsaw puzzle, decide just how puzzled you want to be. Remember, the fewer the pieces, the easier the puzzle!

YOU WILL NEED:
Magazine pictures, large photographs, or old road maps
Scissors
Rubber cement or paste
2 laundry shirt cardboards
Crayons

HERE'S HOW: Find a large magazine picture that you like—some of the advertisements have lovely, colorful landscapes, or perhaps you'll find a portrait of your favorite movie star. Cut out the picture and paste it on the shirt cardboard. If you prefer, paste onto the board a map or a photograph. Trim the cardboard so that it is exactly the same size as the picture. Now cut another cardboard to the same size as the one on which you have your picture. Turn the picture face down, and cover the entire cardboard side with crayon of any one color. This is very important, for if you have a number of jigsaw puzzles around the house, this will help you to distinguish the pieces of one puzzle from those of another. Now carefully cut the cardboard-backed picture into dozens of jagged, curved, uneven pieces. Tiny nail scissors are excellent for this purpose. Store the pieces and the extra whole cardboard together in a bag or envelope, and when you want to assemble your puzzle, use the whole cardboard as a base. Make lots of puzzles, and don't forget to color the back of each one a different color.

TAMBOURINES

This is simple and satisfying, and will keep all junior jumping beans in one place: next to the record player or radio. It will also help develop a sense of rhythm and an awareness of the pleasure of participating in music making.

YOU WILL NEED:
A handful of pennies or tiny bells
2 paper plates or silver-foil plates
A stapler or cellophane tape

HERE'S HOW: Place a dozen pennies (or little round jingle bells, left over from Christmas) on a paper plate. Place another paper plate of the same size upside down on top of the first. Staple or tape the two plates together all around the flat brim, and you've made a marvelous—and musical—tambourine! Hold your tambourine by the brim and shake it or tap it. Incidentally, if you use two silver-foil cake plates (the kind in which frozen cakes and pies are often packaged), the sound will be even brighter. Turn on the record player or radio, and play along!

BUILDING BLOCKS

Don't throw away those empty waxed milk cartons. You haven't milked the last drop out of them yet! They can be washed, cut, pasted, painted, linked, and eventually thrown away with a clear conscience—after all, they're free! Milk and cream cartons with flat tops are ideal for preschool block play. The advertising on the outside won't bother the youngsters at all, but covering the writing can be fun in itself.

YOU WILL NEED:
Milk or cream cartons
Aluminum foil
Cellophane tape
Poster paint
1 teaspoonful soap flakes or detergent
Construction, crepe, or grocery-bag paper
Rubber cement

19

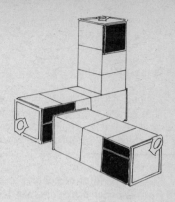

HERE'S HOW: Wrappers of aluminum foil will turn these blocks into glittering silver bricks. Just cover as you would a gift package, and fasten each end with a tiny piece of cellophane tape; or poster paints will stick to the waxed surface if you put a teaspoonful of packaged soap or detergent into the jar of paint before you start; or paper (construction, crepe, or from grocery bags) can be made to adhere, with rubber cement.

Children don't have to be shown how to play with blocks. Leave 'em alone and they'll do what comes naturally.

LINKING BLOCKS

These—as I described them in *Good Housekeeping Magazine*—are more fun (and more challenging) than plain building blocks. They join together with great ease, and the play possibilities are endless. If two square openings are cut in each carton, the blocks can then be linked together, one into another. These blocks can be connected to construct all sorts of shapes and forms, then taken apart and put together again, this time in a completely different way. This is more than just a "keep busy" activity—it is an engrossing project, excellent for developing co-ordination, and imagination too!

MILK-CARTON PUPPET

Here's a puppet that will know (and be able to recite) all the poems and jokes that every child in the house knows! Amazing, isn't it?

YOU WILL NEED:

    1 milk carton
    Pencil
    Scissors
    Paints, brushes and 1 teaspoonful soap flakes or detergent;
         or construction paper and rubber cement; or colored
         plastic tape
    1 knitted sock

HERE'S HOW: Stand a milk carton upright and draw a pencil line all around the middle of the container. Along this line, cut the front and the two sides of the container. Do *not* cut the back. You now have two halves, connected only in back. Open the two halves, and the back will start to bend. Continue to open these two halves in this way until they meet in back, folding the solid back strip in half. The edges of the top and the bottom of the carton are now touching each other. On the other side of the container, you will find two separate pockets. Put your thumb in the bottom pocket, and your other fingers in the top pocket. As you open and close your hand, the top and the bottom separate and come together again. If you draw eyes, nose, and top lip on the top—lower lip and chin on the bottom—you'll have a talking puppet. The features can be painted. Put the soap in the paint, or wipe the brush over a cake of soap before you dip it in the paint. This will make the paint stick to the waxy surface. The features can also be cut out of construction paper and fastened on with rubber cement, or cut out of colored plastic tape and pressed on. I cut the foot off a knitted sock and used the ankle band to cover my arm at the point where it entered the back of the puppet.

 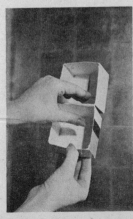

21

TRAINS

YOU WILL NEED:
   Scissors
   1 milk carton
   Pencil
   1 juice glass
   Brass fasteners or pencils
   Paint
   Paper
   Rubber cement

HERE'S HOW: Cut off one side of a milk carton. On this discarded side, trace the outline of the bottom of a juice glass, and in this way cut out four wheels. Holding the carton with the open side facing down, attach the wheels with brass fasteners. If you prefer, two round pencils can be used as the wheel axles. Stick each pencil through one wheel, then through the two sides of the carton, and finally through the second wheel. The train windows and doors can either be painted directly onto the waxed carton or drawn on paper, which is

then rubber-cemented to the carton (see Building Blocks*
for painting and pasting suggestions). Boxcars, for transport-
ing cardboard cargo and paper cutout people, can be made
by placing the open side of the carton on top.

INDIAN VILLAGE

The shape of a pointed paper cup immediately suggests an
Indian tepee, and children of all ages delight in constructing
Indian villages. When you've added the household collection
of tin and plastic soldiers, cowboys, and Indians, your family
will have an Indian village which will be quite a feather in
its cap!

YOU WILL NEED:
  Paper cups (cone-shaped)
  Paints or crayons
  Scissors
  Pencils
  Bits of clay (or gumdrops)

HERE'S HOW: To turn a paper cup into a tepee, decorate the
cup with paint or crayon in any way you wish—solid, striped,
dotted, or wildly illustrated tepees will be acceptable to your
toy Indians if they are okay with you. One small cut will make
an authentic-looking tent flap. Indian settlements need lots of
tepees, so this project should keep everyone settled and busy
for a while. When interest lags in the housing project, try
landscaping the tepee settlement with trees made of pointed
paper cups, pencils, and clay. With green paint or crayon,
cover the entire outer surfaces of a couple of paper cups. Then

stick the eraser end of an equal number of sharpened pencils into separate bits of clay (this will cause the pencils to stand upright). Place each green cup (treetop) over a standing pencil (tree trunk), and then scatter the trees among the tepees.

PAINTING AND EASY SCULPTING

FUNNY BRUSHES

Every household has (and discards) empty bottles and containers with wonderful qualities—the sides or the tops can be squeezed or pressed, to produce a spray; or perhaps the top has a thick brush or comb (for applying home permanents); or it may have a "ball" (for rolling on deodorants). These bottles make delightful paintbrushes and produce surprising effects.

YOU WILL NEED:
> Empty bottles or containers
> Paint or ink
> Kitchen sponge (optional)

HERE'S HOW: Remove the top, clean the bottle, fill with thin paint or ink, replace the top, and experiment! Some bottles have small sponges at the top. These produce a textured effect on paper. If you wish, a discarded kitchen sponge can be used in the same way, to cover a larger area with a textured design.

SPILLPROOF PAINT CONTAINER

When you're dealing with paints, remember that an ounce of prevention is worth a pint of cleaning fluid. Spilled paint is very much like spilled milk. Tears are no help at all!

YOU WILL NEED:
> Glue (Elmer's or Duco)
> A few deep bottle caps from catchup containers
> An old round metal pie tin, or an aluminum-foil disposable pan from a frozen-food package

An empty tuna-fish can, with the top neatly removed
Paints

HERE'S HOW: Glue the deep bottle caps inside the pie tin, around the edge, and glue the tuna-fish tin in the middle. Fill each bottle cap with a little paint of a different color. The tuna-fish tin will hold a few ounces of water.

HOMEMADE FINGER PAINTS

See Window Painting* for the simplest formula for home-made finger paint, using only household items. Here are three slightly different recipes.

YOU WILL NEED:
    Soap flakes
    Concentrated liquid laundry starch
    Poster paints or powdered paint
    Small empty jars with screw tops

HERE'S HOW: Add soap flakes to the liquid starch, until the mixture takes on the desired depth of color (a little will go a long, long way—approximately a half teaspoon of paint to two cups of mixture should do very well).

The next recipe takes a little more effort, but I have found that this formula produces the best finger paint.

YOU WILL NEED:
    1½ cups laundry starch
    1 quart boiling water
    ½ cup talcum powder (optional)
    1½ cups soap flakes
    Small empty jars with screw tops
    ½ teaspoon poster paint or powdered paint per jar
    Wheat paste (optional)

HERE'S HOW: Mix the starch with a little cold water, to form a creamy paste. Add the boiling water and cook until the mixture becomes transparent (it will look rather glassy). Stir it constantly. Add the talcum powder to make the paint smoother. Let the mixture cool a little, and then add the soap flakes and stir until smooth. Let cool and pour the mixture into jars. Into each jar, stir the paint. Put a different color in each jar.

Or, for another good and quick finger-painting mixture, mix

wheat paste with water to a creamy consistency, and then add color.

The ideal paper for finger painting is glossy and non-absorbent. Glazed shelving paper is excellent. If you wish, you can buy commercial finger-paint paper. I like to dampen the paper before I apply the paint. Oilcloth is very fine as a finger-painting surface, for it can be washed and then used again.

MAGIC PAINTING

I love this technique, because it has the quality of "magic."

YOU WILL NEED:
Wax crayons
Paper
Water colors, poster paint, or India ink

HERE'S HOW: Put a crayon design or picture on paper. The crayon should be applied heavily; plenty of white space should be left around the picture or design. Then brush a wash (a very watery solution) of water color, poster paint, or India ink over the entire surface. The crayon will resist the paint, but the rest of the paper area will be covered.

You could, for example, use white wax crayon on white paper, which would, of course, be invisible until you brushed your paint over it.

CLAY DOUGH

Wonderful modeling mediums can be made at home of "homey" materials. A very similar formula is sold, and not inexpensively, either. Save your dough, and make your own!

YOU WILL NEED:
2 cups flour
1 cup salt
2 tablespoons olive oil
Vegetable food coloring

HERE'S HOW: Mix all the ingredients and work them together (knead them) with your hands. Keep the Clay Dough in a plastic bag when it's not being used, and it will last and last.

HARDENING PLAY DOUGH

Here's a modeling mixture that will dry and can then be painted.

YOU WILL NEED:
>   Flour
>   Salt
>   Cool water
>   Laundry shirt cardboard
>   Paint
>   Toothpick or needle (optional)

HERE'S HOW: Mix equal parts of flour and salt. Add enough cool water to make the mixture creamy. Place the final piece of sculpture on a sheet of cardboard, and let it dry and harden before you paint it.

Big beads are fun to shape, paint, and then thread. Use the above formula, roll bits of the mixture into ball shapes, and pierce each with a toothpick (or thread the beads on large needles). When they are dry, remove the toothpick or needle and paint.

CLAY MOSAIC

Clay and crayons can produce a charming combination of color and texture.

YOU WILL NEED:
>   Clay (different colors if you wish)
>   Wax paper
>   Rolling pin
>   Any shallow box top
>   Cooky cutters (optional)
>   Broken bits of crayon, buttons, or bits of broken jewelry

HERE'S HOW: Place a hunk of clay between two sheets of wax paper, and roll it flat. Put the flattened clay in the box top. Then stick broken chips of crayon deep into the clay, to form a picture or design. I used clay of different colors, to simulate the look of a stained-glass window. Mine is a Christmas mosaic. Yours might be flowers, trees, simple animals (such as rabbits or chickens), or just a pretty arrangement of shapes and colors.

Use all available cooky cutters for making lots of shapes out of clay, and utilize buttons and bits of broken jewelry for decorating and making features.

SILVER STATUES

This is an idea of my mother's, and I do think it's a goody!

YOU WILL NEED:
    Modeling clay (of any kind)
    Aluminum foil

HERE'S HOW: Make any kind of clay statue (human, animal, or a lovely abstract shape). Then cover the entire form with aluminum foil. Gently press the foil close to the clay shape, and it will cling to the outline of the statue, giving it the rough, handsome look of hammered metal.

If your clay can be baked, bake it first and then cover it. If your clay is the kind which hardens when exposed to air, let it harden, and then add the silvery "skin."

With clay that hardens (through baking or drying), try shaping the initial of the family name. Let it harden, cover it with foil, and present it to Dad for use as a very personal paperweight. He'll enjoy it so much, he'll *never* throw his weight around!

BALLOON FUN

If you happen to have some balloons around the house, the dreary atmosphere out-of-doors will not be reflected indoors, for there are so many things to do and make with balloons. See the Reindeer Balloon,* the Santa Claus Balloon,* Balloon O'Lantern,* Bal-loonies,* and others pictured on the jacket.

WATER PLAY

Your home has a secret playroom—the bathroom. It's an almost ideal play area, with built-in equipment (requiring only inexpensive supplies), potentialities for exciting and educational activities, and practically indestructible surroundings. Playtime is much more fun when you know that all the mess can be tidied up with very little effort. Here are some play ideas involving children (as many as can comfortably fit) and adults (at least one, with half an eye on the activities).

Right in your bathroom, I'll bet you have a tub. Now bathtubs can be used for taking baths (yes—this can be fun if you bathe with Terry-cloth Puppets* and Soap Snowballs*). Bathtubs are also perfect for sailing boats and playing water games.

PENNY PITCHING

This is an excellent game for two children.

YOU WILL NEED:
    2 saucers of different colors or patterns
    10 or more pennies

HERE'S HOW: Start with half a tubful of water. Each player carefully floats his own ship (saucer) on the surface of the ocean (tub). Then, standing back as far as he can—perhaps at the bathroom door—he gets five chances to drop bombs (pennies) on his opponent's ship. The winner is the contestant

who, after a certain number of attempts (at five pennies each), has scored the greatest number of direct hits. A direct hit is scored only when the penny remains on the plate. This is pretty tricky, because the saucers bounce about and become slippery as their top surfaces get wet. This is a do-it-yourself version of an old carnival game, and is a favorite with youngsters of all ages, so Mother should be given a turn too—she may discover that she's a power-packed penny pitcher!

SAILBOAT

Boats float, and so do waxed cartons. That's where the fun begins!

YOU WILL NEED:
> Waxed containers
> Pencil
> Cellophane tape
> Paper
> Aluminum foil (optional)

HERE'S HOW: Lay a container on its side. Stick a pencil (point down) into the side of the carton that is on top, and tape a triangle of paper to the pencil. That's a bathtub-seaworthy sailboat. The advertising can be covered, if you wish, by wrapping the container in aluminum foil.

CARTON CABIN CRUISER

YOU WILL NEED:
> Scissors
> A waxed milk carton
> A knife
> Colored construction paper and cellophane tape or plastic
>   tape

HERE'S HOW: Cut the container (as indicated by the dotted lines in the illustration) so that about two inches remain in the center to form the cabin. When you finish you will have three sections (see illustration). Cut off the ends of small sections A and B. Drop sections A and B into the hollow in the launch (illustration).

If you want to make your launch really colorful, cover the sections with different-colored construction paper and fasten

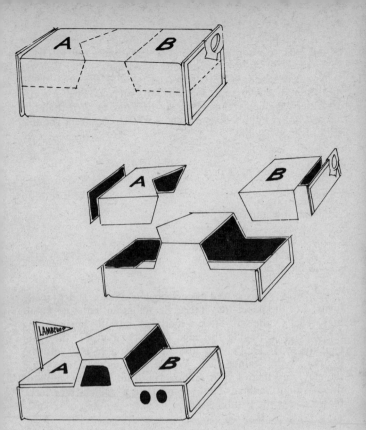

with cellophane tape before dropping them into position. Use black construction paper for portholes and windows. Colored plastic tape is even better than construction paper, for it is waterproof.

Happy sailing!

TUGBOAT

YOU WILL NEED:
    Waxed containers
    Scissors
    Paper toweling
    Rubber cement
    Paper dolls (optional)

HERE'S HOW: Lay the carton on its side and cut out the side that is on top. Push the front end out a little, so that the bow of the boat will come to a point. Cut cardboard rolls (from paper toweling) to the proper height, and with rubber cement, fasten them standing upright to the floor of the boat. They make superb smokestacks for your little tugboat. Two or three of these open boats can be strung together to form bathtub barges. Paper cutout dolls are the perfect passengers for this kind of happy sailing.

WALNUT SAILBOAT

YOU WILL NEED:
    Half a walnut shell
    Scissors
    White paper (typing paper or wax paper)
    A toothpick
    A bit of clay

HERE'S HOW: This is the easiest boat to make, and it really floats! Cut the paper into a triangle, about an inch and a half high. That's your sail! Stick a toothpick into the sail, piercing the paper twice along the edge (near the bottom and again near the top). That's your mast! Press a bit of clay into the bottom of the walnut shell. Wedge the toothpick mast into the clay, and there's your sailboat, in a nutshell! A couple of these Walnut Sailboats could compete in a sailboat race to be blown across the bathtub sea.

FLOATING SOAP BOAT

YOU WILL NEED:
  1 cake floating soap
  4 lollipop sticks or pipe cleaners
  String

HERE'S HOW: Soak a cake of floating soap in warm water to soften it. Push three lollipop sticks or pipe cleaners perpendicularly into the top side of the soap (the middle stick or pipe cleaner should be the highest). Then push the fourth stick or pipe cleaner on an angle into the narrow end of the cake. Tie a piece of string from stick to stick until all four sticks are connected. A couple of these Floating Soap Boats make a beautiful flotilla!

SOAP SNOWBALLS

On some idle, stay-at-home day make a batch of Soap Snowballs,* wrap them in waxed paper (or silver foil), and store them for use in the tub during the months ahead. For instructions, see Chapter VI.

TERRY-CLOTH PUPPETS

For attaining that cleanliness which is next to godliness with the least unpleasantness, make and use Terry-Cloth Puppets. Here are three different types, all fun.

WINKY

YOU WILL NEED:
Pencils
Paper
Scissors
A towel
Straight pins
Needle and thread
Embroidery thread or bits of colored terry cloth from other old towels
Colorfast binding tape (optional)

HERE'S HOW: Loosely trace the outline of your hand on a piece of paper. Keep all your fingers together, so the outline looks like a mitten *without* a thumb. Enlarge the outline about a half inch all around, to allow for a seam. Then cut it out. Fold the towel in half and pin the paper pattern to the towel. Trace the pattern onto the towel and then cut along the outline through the double thickness of towel. You now have two thumbless-mitten shapes. Sew the pieces together along the rounded edges, leaving the bottom part open. Turn inside out and slip it on your hand. Pencil a simple, funny face on the part of the mitten covering the palm of your hand. Make sure one eye straddles the fold in your palm directly under your pinkie. Take off the mitten and either embroider the features (with colorfast thread, please!) or cut them out of colored toweling and sew them in place. Hem the open bottom edge

or bind it with colorfast binding tape. At bath time slip her (or him) on (with the face over the palm of your hand), and when you bend your fingers down, she'll wink at you! She's not fresh—just friendly.

WILLIE TALK

This puppet is not only a helpful washcloth, he's good company.

YOU WILL NEED:
Pencil
Paper
Scissors
A towel
Straight pins
Needle and thread
Embroidery thread or bits of colored terry cloth from other old towels
Colorfast binding tape (optional)

HERE'S HOW: Loosely trace the outline of your hand on a piece of paper. This time keep all fingers together but your thumb. The outline will look just like a mitten. Enlarge the outline about a half inch all around, to allow for a seam. Then cut it out. Fold the towel in half, pin the paper pattern on the towel, and then cut along the outline through the two layers of towel. You now have two mitten shapes. Sew them

together along the rounded edges, leaving the flat bottom part open. Turn the mitten inside out and put it on your hand. With a pencil, draw two eyes and a nose on the part of the mitten covering the back of your hand. The mouth is drawn at the point where the thumb meets the hand, with the top lip on the pointer finger, the lower lip on the thumb. Take off the mitten and either embroider the features with colorfast thread or cut them out of colored toweling and sew them in place. Hem the open edge or bind with colorfast binding tape. Put him on your hand, move your thumb up and down, and watch Willie Talk talk. If you slip a small cake of soap into the mitten and hold it in the palm of your hand, Willie Talk would be delighted personally to scrub your back!

SOAP SILLIES

These are very helpful puppets, for with their two little hands they can hold the soap, turn on the water, and even applaud you, when you've done a good scrub-a-dub job!

YOU WILL NEED:
Tracing paper
Pencil
Scissors
A towel
Straight pins
Needle and thread
Embroidery thread or bits of colored terry cloth from other old towels
Small bits of colored toweling (optional)
Colorfast binding tape (optional)

HERE'S HOW: Draw a rough outline of your child's hand on a

piece of paper, adding an extra thumb as in the puppet outline shown below. Enlarge the pattern a half inch all around. Cut out the enlarged outline. Fold a towel in half, pin the paper shape to the towel, trace the pattern, and then cut through the two layers of towel, along the outline. Sew the pieces together along the rounded edges, leaving only the flat bottom edge open. Turn the puppet inside out. On the round face, lightly pencil features. Embroider them with bright colorfast thread or cut them out of colored toweling and sew them in place. Ears (as on the bunny puppet in the illustration) or hat (as on the clown in the illustration) can be cut out of colored towel, slightly stuffed with small bits of toweling, and sewn in place. Hem the bottom edge or bind with colorfast tape. Now put your pointer finger and your middle finger together into the head, your thumb into one arm, and your ring finger and pinkie into the other arm. This puppet can scratch his head, clap, and even take a bow, so when your youngsters hop into the tub, the Soap Silly can do all the work. With him around, it won't be work; it'll be play.

BATHROOM BUBBLE BLOWFEST

Bubbles intrigue me. The idea that a soap "skin" can contain air is fantastic, and the color, shape, and life span of any given bubble present a real (if ludicrous) challenge.

YOU WILL NEED:
   1–2 children (seated on folded towels on the bathroom
      floor)
   A bowl of warm water
   Soap (yellow soap is excellent)
   A spoon

Any or all of the following:
   A spoonful of sugar
   Glycerine (from the drugstore)

A small kitchen funnel
Soda straws
Empty spools (without the thread)
A cigarette holder
Bubble pipes or rings
Scissors
Vegetable food coloring

There are many different formulas for making strong, beautiful bubbles. Here are some of the easiest.

HERE'S HOW: Rub a cake of yellow soap in a bowl of warm water until there is a heavy lather. With a spoon, remove the lather and even the tiniest bubbles. Then test the solution: Blow a bubble bigger than your fist (see instructions below). Now dip one finger into the soap solution and immediately thrust it into the bubble. If the bubble bursts, the soap mixture is not strong enough. (Rub in some more soap.) A little sugar, added to the soapy water, also helps to make long-lasting bubbles, but the addition of two tablespoons of glycerine makes them so strong they can be bounced and gently batted back and forth like a volleyball.

To blow a bubble, hold either the funnel, soda straw, empty spool, cigarette holder, bubble pipe or ring so that one end of its rests upon the surface of the solution. When it is lifted, you will notice a shiny film across the opening. Blow very gently and the bubble will form. When it is big enough, a sharp jerk will release it. Just for fun, try this. Dunk your closed fist into the soap solution. Open your hand slowly under water while loosening your curved fingers, until your thumb and pointer fingers meet only at the tips and form a ring. Now lift your hand slowly out of the water and hold the finger ring in front of your mouth. Blow into the soap film between your fingers until a big bubble appears.

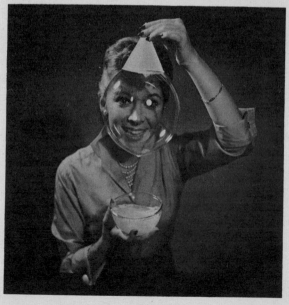

40

To make a soda-straw bubble pipe that really works, cut four tiny slits at one end of the straw. Bend the four sections open just a little (see illustration). Then dip that end into the soapy water and blow!

For colored bubbles, add a few drops of vegetable coloring to your soapy solution. Try it and you'll see why I'm forever blowing bubbles.

DOLL BATHS

Now I don't doubt for a minute that your bathroom also has a sink. Sinks are commonly used for washing hands, but baby dolls like to be washed in the sink too. And certain water puppets play very happily under faucets.

Any household that includes a young girl also includes a few dolls that could use a bath. A large basin half filled with sudsy water, another filled with clear water, a small stiff brush, a towel, a girl, and some dolls—these are the necessary ingredients for an entire afternoon of doll grooming and feminine fussing. After the dolls are sparkling, try giving the dolls' clothing a scrub-a-dub in the tub. It's good training, good fun, and a good wet way to spend a rainy day.

MR. I. GLASS

This is the silliest sink puppet I know.

YOU WILL NEED:
    A paper cup with a handle
    A pencil

HERE'S HOW: Start with a paper cup with a handle. The handle consists of two circular flaps attached to the cup (and to each other) by a flat strip of cardboard. Open the two flaps until they look like a pair of eyeglasses. Draw two eyes inside the glasses and a round mouth under the connecting flap strip of cardboard. Push a pencil through the mouth circle, and when you have made a hole, wriggle the pencil around a little to enlarge the mouth opening. You will find that if you hold Mr. I. Glass under a faucet he will willingly drink the water (through the hole in the top of his head), but it will pour out of his mouth in a very funny way—guess he's just not thirsty!

ACTIVE GAMES

Some of these use items that you find in your kitchen, and can be enjoyed either alone or with other children.

FLYING SAUCERS

YOU WILL NEED:
    Wire hanger
    String
    Cellophane tape
    Small paper plates (or aluminum-foil plates from frozen-food packages)

HERE'S HOW: Pull down the straight bottom rung of a wire hanger, until the hanger looks something like a circle with a hook on top. Tie a piece of string to the hook and tape the end of the string to the top of an open doorway. Now stand across the room and try to fly your saucers through the circle. If you hold the plate flat and skim it across the room, it will sail just beautifully! If you wish, make a realistic flying saucer by taping, gluing, or stapling two paper plates together. Hold them so that they face each other, and attach them around the rim. Give yourself five points for each successful trip.

RINGTOSS

YOU WILL NEED:
    Paper plates
    Scissors

43

Cellophane tape
4 pennies
Kitchen chair
Crayon

HERE'S HOW: Start with a couple of paper plates of any size, and cut away the inner surface of each plate, leaving only the outer circle, the flat, firm brim (generally this stiff brim is fluted or ridged). Tape the pennies to the underside of each cardboard rim (the pennies should be spaced evenly around the ring). This will give the paper ring a feeling of weight, and when tossed, it will sail in a very satisfying manner.

Turn a kitchen chair upside down so that the four legs stick up into the air but lean slightly toward you. The aim of the game is to toss the rings onto the legs of the chair. If two or more youngsters are playing, each participant should have three rings marked in crayon with his name.

FEED THE CAT

If you have a paper plate, a pair of scissors, a crayon, and a few Ping-pong balls handy, see the Feed the Cat* game in Chapter X.

HOLE-IN-THE-POCKET BALL

This is a junior basketball game.

YOU WILL NEED:
Cellophane tape
Paper cup
Scissors
Aluminum foil

HERE'S HOW: Tape a paper cup to the wall, just a wee bit out of the player's reach. If the cup comes to a point, cut off about one inch of the bottom, including the point; if the cup has a flat bottom, remove it. An ideal ball can be made by crumpling a piece of aluminum foil until it is the size of a large marble—round, but not too firmly packed. "Shoot" for the "basket" from a few feet away.

PICK UP STICKS

Hold a fistful of toothpicks tightly in your hand. Put your fist on the table (or on the floor), with the toothpicks standing upright. Suddenly, release your grasp on the bundle of toothpicks, open your fingers, and let the toothpicks fall where they may. The fun of the game is in removing one "pick up stick" (toothpick) at a time, without moving any of the other toothpicks. A spare toothpick may be used to help separate (careful now!) the "pick up sticks" that are lying near or on top of one another.

If you have colored toothpicks, give each color a different point value.

BOWLING

YOU WILL NEED:
   Waxed milk cartons
   Ball

HERE'S HOW: Simply stand a number of waxed milk cartons together (perhaps in a V formation) and roll a ball. Whoever can knock down all the pins (cartons) in the least number of tries is the winner.

THE INNER CIRCLE GAME

YOU WILL NEED:
   Cup or small custard bowl
   Medium-sized bowl
   Large mixing bowl
   Beans or buttons

HERE'S HOW: Place a cup (or a small custard bowl) inside a medium-sized bowl. Now put this bowl into a large mixing bowl. Place the nest of bowls on the table or on the floor. Stand back a few feet and pitch beans into the bowls. A bean in the biggest bowl is worth five points, in the middle bowl, ten points, and in the cup, fifteen points. Buttons can be used in place of beans.

LOTS OF POTS

YOU WILL NEED:
   Lots of pots
   Wax crayon
   Pennies

45

HERE'S HOW: Next to one another, place all the pots you can find in a corner on the kitchen floor. With a wax crayon, write "5" on the sides of all the biggest pots, "10" on all the medium-sized ones, and "15" on the baby pots. Then toss pennies, one at a time, into the group of pots, and see how many points you can get!

You'll find everything you need for the following games in your dresser drawers, toy cabinets, or clothes closets. These, too, are games for one child or more.

SOCK TOSS

This game should please Mother and the children, because it has all the pleasures of a ball game with none of the "at home" problems of furniture breakage.

YOU WILL NEED:
    2–3 pairs shoes: Dad's, Mom's and children's
    3 pairs men's socks
    Rubber bands

HERE'S HOW: Dig into the family clothes closets and pull out two or three pairs each of Dad's, Mom's, and children's shoes. Line them up against a wall in three rows—Dad's nearest the wall, Mom's in front of Dad's, and then the children's shoes in the very first row, closest to the player or players. Roll three pairs of men's socks tightly into a ball and put a rubber band around each sock-ball. Toss the sock-balls, one at a time, into the openings of the shoes. The opening is, of course, not the hole you may have in the sole, but the hole into which you put your foot! Dad's shoes have the biggest openings, and so they are worth the fewest points. The children's shoes are the toughest targets, and so they get the greatest number of points.

CLOTHESPIN BOWLING

YOU WILL NEED:
    Clothespins
    Ball
    Stuffed dolls or animals (optional)

HERE'S HOW: Stand the flat-topped clothespins upside down

on their little heads. On the floor, place ten clothespins in a bowling V, with four in the back row, three in the next, two in front of them, and one in front, forming the very point of the V. Stand about six feet away, roll the ball toward the bowling "pins," and try to knock down as many as you can. If they all go down at once, it's a strike," worth twenty-five points. If only one or a few go down, they're worth two points each. If you can't find clothespins, use large stuffed dolls and animals. Line them up, roll the ball, and watch them fall! I'm sure your stuffed creatures won't mind—I've played this game on TV often, and mine have never uttered a word of complaint!

BIDDIE BASKETBALL

YOU WILL NEED:
    Cellophane or adhesive tape
    Thimble
    Beans or dried peas

HERE'S HOW: At the eye level of the player or players, tape a thimble to the wall with cellophane or adhesive tape. Stand about three feet away from the wall, and try to get "baskets" by tossing beans or dried green peas into the thimble. Every time you get a bean into the "basket," you get five points, but make sure that you don't come any closer to the thimble than three feet. Remember, this doesn't work according to basketball rules, and so no fair shooting from directly under the basket!

Here are a group of games for two or more children that are guaranteed to put more play in your playroom on a rainy day.

JUNIOR JAVELIN THROW

YOU WILL NEED:
    Straws
    Various-colored crayons

HERE'S HOW: If you hold a straw between the tips of your thumb and pointer fingers, draw your hand back over your shoulder, and throw the straw like a javelin, it will whiz across the room in a funny way. Each contestant gets three straws and one crayon (every player gets a crayon of a different color). On his straws, he marks a dot of his color, so that the players can tell to whom the winning straw belongs. Then both (or all) the players line up along the wall at one side of the room, and they throw their straw javelins. The straw that sails the farthest is the winner of that set and is worth one point. You play until one contestant has twenty-five points.

POTLUCK

Have your plans for the day gone to pot? Why fight it? Get out some pots and play away.

YOU WILL NEED:
  Cooking pots with handles (1 for each player)
  Bean bags

HERE'S HOW: The players stand a small distance from one another. Each holds a cooking pot by the handle. The hand not holding the pot is placed behind each player's back. The beanbag is then tossed from pot to pot. Only the pot may be used to toss or catch the beanbag. When you don't succeed in catching the bag, and it falls to the ground, you get a point. When one contestant gets fifteen points the game is over, and whoever has the lowest score is the winner.

THE FLYING FEATHER

Two children can play this game, or two teams of children. The players (or teams of players) stand at opposite ends of a table. A feather is set in the center of the table, and the contestants try to blow the feather off their opponents' end of the table. When the feather blows off one side, the player (or players) on the other side gets a point. When a contestant (or team) gets fifteen points, the game is over.

FUN WITH FUNNELS

You will probably find some funnels in the kitchen drawers, and they're the basis of a funny balloon game. This game is similar to the Potluck* game, except that Potluck is a catching game and this one is really a balancing game.

48

YOU WILL NEED:

Funnels (1 for each player)
1 inflated balloon

HERE'S HOW: Each player holds a funnel by the neck, with the wide mouth on top. A balloon is tossed from player to player, and caught in the wide opening of the funnel. The balloon is tossed and caught, using only the funnel—never is it to be touched by human hands (which means, of course, if you have a monkey, he can use his hands, and you'll obviously win, hands down)! You get a point when you do *not* catch the balloon in your funnel, and it falls to the ground. When any player reaches ten points, the game is over, and the contestant with the *fewest* points is the winner.

A BALLOON, A SPOON, AND YOU

YOU WILL NEED:

2 chairs
1 long string
2 tablespoons (soupspoons)
1 inflated balloon

HERE'S HOW: Place the two chairs pretty far apart, and stretch the string from chair to chair (tie the ends of the strings to the backs of the chairs). The players (or teams) stand on opposite sides of the string, with their spoons in their hands. The point of this balloon tennis game—and the way to get points in this game—is to hit the ball (balloon) with your racket (spoon) over the net (string) into your opponent's court (his side of the string), so that he cannot return it to you. When he misses, and the balloon hits the floor on his side of the court, you get a point. The first player to get twenty points is the winner, with no strings attached!

BUTTON BULL'S-EYE BOARD

YOU WILL NEED:

Scissors
1 large cardboard grocery carton
Crayons
1 dinner plate
1 saucer
1 cup
Buttons (of any kind)

49

HERE'S HOW: Cut off the largest side of a cardboard grocery carton and lay the sheet of cardboard on a table. At one end, trace the outline of a dinner plate. Inside that circle, trace the shape of a saucer. Within these two circles, trace the rim of a cup, and put a dot in the very center. That's your bull's-eye! Use bright crayons for your outlines. Give each circle a point value (perhaps fifteen points for the dot, ten for the circle, five for the saucer, and one point for the dinner plate). Then, standing at the opposite end of the cardboard, take turns sliding buttons toward the bull's-eye.

Paper-Cup Pool* is as much fun on a kitchen table as it is in the back yard.

CHAPTER II

Fun on a Sick-in-Bed Day

I've found that there are different kinds of sick-in-bed days, and each presents a unique and specific challenge.

There are those days when the patient is quite sick, and the best you can do is to make him comfortable. If you're lucky, after a while the patient will feel a little better, and on days like these, rest is generally called for, and he must be kept quiet and at ease. Then, when the patient becomes an impatient patient, he is definitely on the road to recovery, and your job is to keep him interested, not too active, and in bed. The final recuperative period is the most exhausting period for Mother. The trick at this time is to involve the ex-patient in activities that he can do *alone*, while Mother rests! First let's make the patient comfortable, and *then* we'll make him happy.

PATIENT COMFORT

YOU WILL NEED:
Any or all of the following:
    A bridge table
    Cellophane or thumbtacks
    An empty shoe bag
    Books, pencils, crayons, pads, dolls, toy soldiers, wooden cars, tissues
    Medicines
    A thermometer
    An empty paper bag
    A clean cardboard grocery carton
    Scissors

HERE'S HOW: Place a bridge table next to the bed. With tape or thumbtacks, hang an empty shoe bag from the side of the table. Each pocket will hold a few minutes' pleasure, and this will keep a day's entertainment right at his fingertips. Insert small books, pencils and crayons, pads, tiny dolls, toy soldiers, wooden cars, tissues, medicines, thermometer, and all other necessary small items into the handy separate compartments.

Tape an empty paper bag to the side of the table, to hold used tissues and scraps of paper.

BED TRAY

Make a large sturdy bed tray out of the grocery carton. Remove the top flaps and cut a kneehole on each side of the carton. Then turn the carton upside down, so that the flat bottom is on *top*, place the kneeholes over the patient's knees, and he'll have a tray for mealtime (no more balancing of food trays). This is also a perfect worktable for crayoning and playing with small toys.

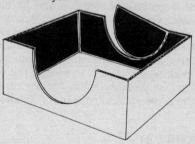

READING TRAY

Reading matter will require a bit of consideration. When you feel poorly, your reading level can drop—sometimes more than just a few notches. If the patient is allowed to read, but shows no interest in books recommended for his age level, make available a book or two of a simpler nature. These easier books may satisfy him at the moment, and when he recuperates, he'll revert to his usual reading level.

Some grown-ups love to talk about their operations. Sick children can sometimes get similar relief and satisfaction from books about people and animals who are or have been ill. For example, look for the wonderful story *Madeline*, by Ludwig Bemelmans. This little French girl had an appendectomy which made her the envy of all her classmates.

Another excellent book, prepared under the supervision of a doctor (Lester L. Coleman, M.D.) is *A Visit to the Hospital* by Francine Chase. Your local librarian can help you to find other books of this nature.

READING STAND

YOU WILL NEED:
    A big flat suit box
    Razor blade
    Pencil

HERE'S HOW: Remove the lid of the box and turn it upside down, with the open part facing *up*. In the middle of each of the two longer side panels of the lid, cut a slit. Turn the box upside down again (with the open part now facing *down*) and draw a line across the back of the box top from slit to slit. Score this line—run over it lightly with a razor blade, but do not cut through the cardboard. Bend the lid neatly in half and place the folded box top into the bottom half of the box (see illustrations). Brace the lid crosswise against the longer sides of the box. It will remain in this raised position and a book will stay propped up against your homemade bookrest in a most convenient manner!

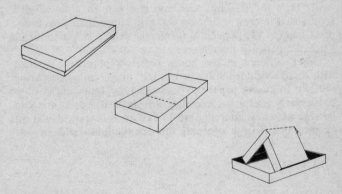

FISH-A-VISION

Television is often a strain on the eyes when you're ill. (Sometimes this is even true when you're well!) For pleasant passive viewing, put a bowl of goldfish beside the TV set.

Their gentle effortless movements are relaxing and offer an ever-changing picture.

MAGIC MOTHBALLS

These will catch the patient's eye.

YOU WILL NEED:
   A glass bowl or jar
   1 cup water
   1 cup vinegar
   1 teaspoon moistened baking soda
   4-5 mothballs (whole or flaked)
   A tiny china figure (optional)

HERE'S HOW: Mix the water and vinegar, and slowly add the moistened baking soda. Drop in the mothballs. As the bubbles of carbon dioxide form around the mothballs, they will become buoyant, and the balls will magically rise to the surface. Then the bubbles will break, and the mothballs will sink to the bottom of the jar. This cycle will repeat itself almost endlessly. If you use flakes instead of mothballs, it will look as though a snowstorm is taking place in the bowl (or jar). A tiny china figure placed on the bottom will complete your snow scene.

In the care and feeding of a sick person, the care is often easier than the feeding. Anything that can be done to give food visual interest and color will help tempt tired taste buds. See Chapters VI, IX, and X for dinner delicacies which might catch the patient's interest.

Other children in the house (often kept out of contact with their bedridden sister or brother) might enjoy preparing the two following paper-tray treats. I have found these trays particularly useful because they are made of paper and can be thrown away after the meal. This is an excellent way of keeping illness from sweeping through the household!

SILLY SUSAN

YOU WILL NEED:
   3 paper plates (of graduated sizes, if possible, otherwise any available plates will do)
   Rubber cement or glue
   Empty thread spools (these too should be of graduated sizes, if possible)

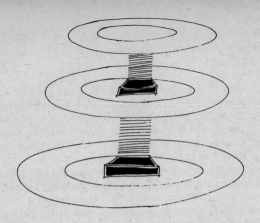

HERE'S HOW: In the center of the bottom (largest) plate, glue or cement the biggest spool. On top of that spool, cement the medium-sized plate, then the medium-sized spool, and, last of all, the tiniest plate.

Serve the various courses of the snack (or lunch) on the different levels—perhaps a sandwich on the bottom plate, a salad (served "finger-food" style) in the middle, and a cooky or a sweet on the top.

Or you can make a Pretty Plate.*

PLANTS

Place a plant or two on the bridge table next to the bed. Novel, playful plantings are, of course, more intriguing to a child and certainly require no more effort or expense. Here are a few gay gardens that will brighten up a sickroom.

DREAM HOUSE

Perhaps you've talked about building a dream house. Now you can do it yourself.

YOU WILL NEED:
An empty cigar box
Aluminum foil
Soil
Scissors

Paper
Crayons or picture of house from magazine (optional)
Rubber cement, glue, or paste
Seeds (grass or flower)

HERE'S HOW: Cover the bottom of the cigar box with aluminum foil, inside and out. Fill the box with soil, cut out a sheet of paper to fit the inside of the lid, and draw a picture of a house (your dream house) on the paper. (If you wish, you may cut a house out of a magazine picture and paste it on the paper.) Paste the paper with the house upon it to the inside of the lid of the cigar box. Put the box on the bed table, with the lid standing upright. Plant a few seeds (grass seeds are marvelous and grow to a wonderful height in just a few days) and you'll have your dream house—complete with a front lawn! P.S. You'll get no crab grass, but don't forget to water your lawn and trim it with a pair of fingernail scissors.

KITCHEN CLIPPINGS

My mother is a schoolteacher, and she has always brightened her classroom and her own kitchen with lovely foliage and flowers, grown from kitchen cuttings.

YOU WILL NEED:
Beets and/or radishes, carrots, potatoes
Pebbles (optional)
Shallow plate of water
Toothpicks
Glass of water

HERE'S HOW: Remove the greenery plus the top inch of beets, radishes, or carrots, and place them on pebbles in a shallow plate of water. Or try potatoes and sweet potatoes, which grow long and leafy vines. Stick two toothpicks into the potato, one on each side (the toothpicks should be placed near the narrow middle of the potato, opposite each other). Half fill a tumbler with water and place the potato into the tumbler so that the toothpicks rest against the lip of the glass and prevent the potato from being submerged. If about one third of the potato is in the water, the plant will flourish.

A SIMPLE SEED BED

Here is an excellent way to cultivate small green thumbs.

YOU WILL NEED:

A waxed milk carton
Scissors
Soil
Seeds (for best results, lima-bean or date)

HERE'S HOW: Lay a waxed milk carton on its side and remove the long side panel that is now on top. Fill the container with moist soil and add seeds. Try lima-bean or date seeds for quick and pretty results.

Art activities are very satisfying and not at all physically demanding. I don't think paints and patients go together: half of the masterpiece usually winds up on the paper; the other half, on the bedclothes. Instead, try crayon crafts. Here are some tricks and tools of the trade.

CRAYONING

YOU WILL NEED:

Crayons (jumbo for young children, standard-size for older children)
Large sheets of paper
Small window screen, sandpaper, or corrugated cardboard (optional)
Cardboard cutouts (optional)
A tissue

HERE'S HOW: Since crayoning means so much more than just "drawing" with crayons, or filling in pre-drawn pictures, try removing the paper wrapper from a stick of crayon and using the entire side of the crayon held flat against the paper. The effect is quite exciting. Or place things which have texture (a small window screen, a piece of rough sandpaper, corrugated cardboard, and so forth) under the paper, and rub the side of the crayon over this sheet. Cardboard cutouts, either home-made or from commercial cutout books, can be used as stencils. Place the cutout under the paper and rub the side of the crayon over this shape.

A jewel-like quality can be achieved by polishing the crayoned surface gently with a tissue.

CRAYON SCRATCHWORK

Here's some etching worth trying.

YOU WILL NEED:
   Paper
   Crayons
   Toothpick, bobby pin, or orange stick

HERE'S HOW: Cover a sheet of paper completely with heavy areas of various bright crayon colors. When the entire sheet is covered, crayon over the colored surface with black. When the sheet is totally covered with the top layer of black crayon, etch or scratch off a design—using a toothpick, bobby pin, fingernail, or orange stick. As you take off the top layer of color, the bottom layer will show through where it has been etched. This creates a very delicate and lovely effect.

CRAYON CARBON PAPER

   This can be used over and over.

HERE'S HOW: Cover a sheet of paper with a heavy coat of crayon color. Use lots of different colors on different parts of the paper. Put this paper *face down* on top of another sheet of paper. Draw or write on the clean side of the crayoned sheet (the clean side is, of course, on top and facing you). Your picture or writing will transfer to the bottom sheet in a random, multicolored pattern. Add more color to the crayon carbon when needed.

   If there is to be a prolonged period of recovery, the youngster can fill the days by making curtains and bedspreads of decorative material for a doll house, or large ones to brighten the sickroom.

YOU WILL NEED:
   Thumbtacks
   A smooth, light-colored, washable fabric (an old sheet
      would be perfect)
   A board (perhaps a breadboard)
   A pencil
   Crayons
   2 sheets of wax paper
   A hot iron

HERE'S HOW: Tack the fabric to a board. With pencil, draw the pattern or picture you wish (perhaps a border design), then go over your pencil lines with crayon and fill in the necessary areas in the picture. Let the crayon follow the weave of the cloth. To "set" the colors, place the fabric between two sheets of wax paper and apply a hot iron. Don't slide the iron over the paper—lift it carefully between "applications."

Between the bed sheets, crumbled crayons are second only to cracker crumbs in nuisance value. Turn Mr. I. Glass* into a crayon container. This funny fellow will be the guardian of these colored bits of wax crayons—the keeper of the pieces.

FEELIES

This is another form of that cut-and-paste art technique called "collage," and it helps to develop a sense of texture as well as of color and shape. This is a good way to teach children about how things feel, but it should be done in such

a way that the child can give his *own* impression of the feeling. All kinds of materials—fabric, textured papers, pieces of old fur, etc., can be used to create these pictures.

Ask the youngster how the materials feel to him, and then encourage him to make a picture, using other materials that feel the same way, or combining these materials with different ones of contrasting texture.

My Feelie was made of velvet pasted on a felt background, and the tips of your fingers can "see" this cat almost as clearly as can your eyes.

NOTEBOOK COVERS

Many bedridden youngsters eagerly look forward to the day when they will be able to return to school. Actively preparing for that day will hasten its arrival.

Here is a daisy of a notebook cover to be made now—used later!

YOU WILL NEED:
>   Rubber cement
>   An inexpensive hard-covered school notebook
>   Fabric (any scrap large enough to cover the book)
>   Scissors
>   Bits of solid, not patterned, fabric or felt in 2 or 3
>   colors

HERE'S HOW: Brush some rubber cement over the front and back covers of the notebook and then cover them with the fabric as you would with paper. Cut any simple outline you wish out of the felt or the solid fabric (a butterfly, an apple, or perhaps a flower). Then cut the small details of the object out of felt or fabric of a contrasting color (the dots for the butterfly's wings, the leaf on the apple, or the stem, the leaves and center of the flower). The best effect can be achieved with the greatest number of layers—as you add these colorful details one on top of another, you also add depth, dimension, and texture to the picture. When you've cut all the necessary pieces, cement these felt appliqués to the front cover of the book.

I use this notebook in the kitchen to hold my recipes, and it gives me a wee bit of pleasure every time I pick it up.

A lonely child needs someone besides Mother with whom he can talk, read, play, and pretend! Puppets are such good listeners—such excellent playmates—so here are some simple paper puppet toys for you to make and enjoy.

STARVING SPAGHETTI MAN

This is the silliest toy, and I'm a bit ashamed to say that it makes me giggle every time I see it. I've used it on television, and it always evokes a flood of "do-it-again" mail.

YOU WILL NEED:
   A large sheet of paper
   Crayons
   Scissors or a sharp pencil
   A small ball of wool or string

HERE'S HOW: Starting at the top of the paper, draw a face with a round, round mouth. Below the face draw a napkin, tied around the neck. Add two hands, holding a fork and knife. Then draw a straight line across the paper, to indicate the edge of the table. On the table draw a plate, and lots and lots of wiggly lines on the plate. That's spaghetti! Make two holes (with a sharp pencil or the point of the scissors), one in the plate, and the second in the Spaghetti Man's mouth. Now thread the loose end of the wool or string into the "plate" hole, entering the hole from the back of the picture and coming out in front. Extend the yarn in front of the picture up to the mouth hole (as in illustration) and insert the end of the wool into his open mouth. Pull it out in back. As you pull and pull and pull, your Starving Spaghetti Man will eat and eat and eat! I like best the moment when you get to the end of the wool and he slurps in the last strand of the spaghetti.

FLAPPER THE BUNNY

This toy bunny flaps his ears.

YOU WILL NEED:
    A square piece of paper
    Crayons
    Scissors

HERE'S HOW: Fold a square of paper diagonally in half (corner to corner, like a diaper). You now have a triangle. Fold the

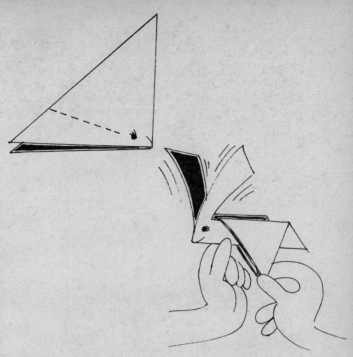

triangle in half again. Your paper should look like mine (see illustration). Draw a bunny's face in the folded corner of the triangle, and cut through all four thicknesses, as indicated by the dotted line in the illustration. The front flaps will be the ears. Fold down the four back flaps, two on one side and two on the other. Hold the corners of the back flaps, pull gently, and Flapper the Bunny will show you how he got his name.

CUPPET

Here's a simple puppet which I described in *Good House-keeping Magazine*.

YOU WILL NEED:
    A paper cup
    Crayons
    Pencil or scissors
    Paper napkin or tissue

HERE'S HOW: On the side of the cup, crayon a face (two eyes, a nose, and a mouth). If the cup has a flat bottom, punch a hole (with a pencil) large enough for a child's index finger. If the cup is cone-shaped, cut off about half an inch from the bottom, including the point, until the child's finger fits into the hole. His index finger, held upright, moves the puppet's head, while the thumb and middle fingers become the hands. Drape a paper napkin or tissue over the hand (held in this three-fingered position) and then stick the cup over the napkin onto the index finger. A puppet pal like this would love to listen to your youngster's favorite story, and be introduced to his toys, records, and other members of the family. This will provide a happy and busy "let's pretend" activity.

JILL-IN-THE-BAG MARIONETTE

This puppet will dance to beat the band (and that band can consist of thirty-six union musicians on television or one humming youngster in bed).

YOU WILL NEED:
  A paper bag
  Crayon
  Scissors
  String

HERE'S HOW: Hold the bag upside down with the open part toward the floor. Draw a face near the fold at the top of the bag. Decide where the neck is going to be, and cut the entire area of the bag below the neck into thin strips. Tie a string around the neck—good and tight. Pull out a few strands on each side, for arms (cut to arm length). Tie string near the end of each "arm" bundle for wrists. Leave an extra length of string attached to each wrist, so you can make your Jill-in-the-Bag bounce about! Tie a string at the waist. To make a Jack-in-the-Bag, separate the strips below the waist into two equal bundles and tie, for legs.

The following games are perfect for slightly sick, badly bored youngsters who must stay in bed.

BUTTON-IN-THE-BUCKET GAME

YOU WILL NEED:

   4-6 milk cartons
   Scissors or knife
   Brass paper fasteners
   Laundry shirt cardboard
   Crayon
   Beans, buttons, or pennies

HERE'S HOW: Cut the cartons in half and throw away the tops. Fasten the bottoms of these open carton cups to the shirt cardboard with paper fasteners. Beside each, in crayon, write a different number. Now each cup is worth a certain number of points. Place the cardboard (with the cups on it) on the floor a few feet from the side of the bed. Give the patient a handful of beans, buttons, or pennies and let him pitch them into the cup one by one. He can play against a visiting friend, standing an equal distance from the cardboard. In this way, the sick child will have company, and the healthy one will be kept a substantial distance from the bed. The youngster who gets the most points wins.

CARTON CUP CATCH

YOU WILL NEED:
- A cardboard grocery carton
- Crayons
- Paper cups (or cottage-cheese containers)
- Scissors
- Rubber bands
- A number of pairs of children's socks or small rubber balls.

HERE'S HOW: On the bottom of the grocery carton, draw four to six circles, tracing the wide mouths of the paper cups or cheese containers. Cut out the circles, but make the holes a bit *smaller* than the circles you have drawn. Insert the cups or containers into the holes, and they will become "pockets," held in place by their wide openings, which are a little bigger than the holes into which they are inserted. Crayon a number inside each "pocket," and prop the carton against the footboard of the bed. Wrap a rubber band two or three times around each rolled pair of children's socks. These will be the "balls." (Small rubber balls will do as well.) Throw the balls, and keep track of your score!

I hope that some of these stay-in-bed-play-in-bed ideas will make laughter the only contagious element in the sickroom.

CHAPTER III

Fun Outdoors on a Sunny Day

BACK-YARD PLAY

A sunny day means outdoor play. Now perhaps all that means to you is that once again you'll have to worry about the younger members of the family who keep straying from the safety of the back yard.

Well, you can catch more flies with honey than you can with flypaper, and I'm pretty sure that the youngsters will stick close to the yard if you suggest a honey of a game (or two) for them to play, within sight and sound of your door. There's so much to do, so many playful activities that they had to stay away from during the winter because of the danger of staining, scratching, or shattering the furniture—and Mother's nerves!

If your back yard has a fence, a garage door, or a wall without low windows, try these.

SNOWBALL BULL'S-EYE

YOU WILL NEED:
Paintbrush (make it a big one)
Bucket or pail
Soap or detergent
Water
Sheet of cardboard (optional)

HERE'S HOW: On the garage door, wall, or back-yard fence, draw a large bull's-eye with a paintbrush dipped in soft suds, and you'll have a fine target for snowball throwing (see Bobbing Balloons* for directions). These snowballs wouldn't

be at home in the North Pole, though, for they're made of
soap or detergent, beaten to a claylike consistency with a
minimum of water. You can also attach a sheet of cardboard,
from a large grocery carton, to a tree, and then draw the target
on the cardboard.

FANCY FENCING

Tom Sawyer won't have a thing on you if you whitewash
your fence or the side of your house. The only difference is
that in this case the whitewash is a bucket of suds (see directions above). And just in case Dad prefers his fence (or
house) dark brown, the garden hose will erase the suds-
whitewash in a jiffy.

If your community is suddenly hit by one of those "so hot
you can fry eggs on the sidewalk" days—don't do it! The
youngsters can amuse themselves (and keep cool) right in the
back yard.
Drown your hot-weather problems with outdoor water play,
and don't let the fact that you haven't got a pool dampen
your spirits. Water can be almost as much fun to play *with*
as it is to play *in!*

SUMMER SNOW MEN

YOU WILL NEED:
>   Bucket of whipped snow (directions above)
>   At least 2 young children in bathing suits
>   Garden hose

HERE'S HOW: Let the youngsters turn one another into snow men. This is so much fun they won't even realize they are getting clean! When they are coated with suds right up to the neck, a garden hose will magically melt the "snow"!

BUBBLE BLOWFEST

YOU WILL NEED:
>   Soap
>   Water
>   Bubble pipes

HERE'S HOW: Spread your soap, water, and bubble pipes out on the grass and bubble away! For funny bubbleblowing suggestions see Bathroom Blowfest.*

71

RUBBER RIVER RACING

YOU WILL NEED:
   An old rubber tire
   A sharp knife
   Water
   Soap or detergent

HERE'S HOW: Cut the tire in half (the long way, so that you still have a circle). Fill the hollow section with water and add a little soap or detergent. Stir the water a bit, and you'll have real whitecaps and waves. The Walnut Sailboats* are perfect for Rubber River Racing. Miniature Floating Soap Boats* are fun, if they are made of small pieces of floating soap, in which case toothpicks should be substituted for the lollipop sticks.

SWIMMING-POOL SAILBOATS

If you do happen to have a pool in the back yard (even a tiny plastic wading pool), you can easily make Waxed-Carton Boats.*

"JUST-LIKE-MOTHER" YARD PLAY

Small girls who have watched Mother bake cakes are enchanted with simple kitchen equipment such as mixing bowls and egg beaters.

YOU WILL NEED:
   Soap or detergent
   Mixing bowl
   Water
   Egg beater
   Cake tin
   Spatula

HERE'S HOW: Put a handful of soap or detergent in a bowl, add a little water, and set it out on the grass in the back yard. Whipping the bit of liquid into a mass of suds is fun. When the "frosting" is ready, give your "little mother" a cake tin and a spatula. She'll spend another happy half hour "icing" her cake. It will look good enough to eat, but please—don't!

A hot day is the ideal time for a young lady to give her dolls the bath they so badly need—don't they always? Put a shallow water basin out on the grass with a bar of soap, a kitchen sponge, and several small towels. I am sure lots of other toys could use a sponging too, and a stuffed Teddy bear, scrubbed, hung on the clothesline to dry, and then brushed with a clean hairbrush will look as good as new.

If you have a clothesline stretching across your yard, or two trees (or fences) between which you can hang a rope or string, you've a very versatile piece of play equipment right at your fingertips (and incidentally, it should be within easy reach of the children's fingertips too). These games are not above their heads: the clothesline shouldn't be either.

PEBBLE PITCH

YOU WILL NEED:
Clothesline
Big pots and pans, with holes or rings in handles
String
Chalk
Pebbles, beanbags, or small balls

HERE'S HOW: Hang a row of the pots and pans on the clothesline by looping a piece of string through each hole or ring in the handle and then tying the string to the clothesline. Decide on which side of the clothesline you are going to stand, and hang the pots so that the bottoms are facing you. On each bottom, in chalk, write a number. The biggest pots should have the smallest point value, and vice versa. Then stand back and pitch pebbles, beanbags, or small balls at the hanging array of pots and pans. Every time you get a "hit," you receive whatever number of points is marked on that particular pot.

NUGGET IN THE BUCKET

This is a variation on the Pebble Pitch* (above). Instead of hanging the pot by the hole in the handle, in this game you hang only things that have round handles (connected on both ends), such as sand pails, shopping bags, kettles, wash buckets, etc.

The suspended object hangs in an upright position, and when you pitch a pebble at the pail or bucket, it should land *in* the receptacle—and remain there! The aim of the game is to place one pebble or beanbag in each hanging object. The closer you get, the easier this becomes, so keep your distance!

73

SHEET SHOOT

In this game, you don't really shoot the sheet, you shoot at a hole or holes in the sheet.

YOU WILL NEED:
    1 old sheet
    Clothesline
    Clothespins (optional)
    Heavy stones
    Scissors
    Crayon
    Balls or beanbags

HERE'S HOW: Drape an old sheet over the clothesline and attach it firmly with a number of clothespins. Secure the bottom of the sheet to the ground with a few well-placed heavy stones. Cut as many holes as you wish in the sheet. Above each hole, crayon a number. Then stand a few feet away and pitch balls or beanbags through the holes. This is a marvelous old-time carnival game, and it can be varied for back-yard parties by crayoning a big clown's face on the sheet and cutting only three holes—two for the eyes and one big one for the mouth.

SHEET SHOW

Use the sheet, hung over the line in this way, as the curtain for hand puppet play. The puppeteer stands hidden behind the sheet, with his hands held above his head, and the puppets dance along the clothesline! See Cuppet,* Winkie,* Willie Talk,* Soap Sillies,* and Milk-Cotton Puppet.*

BALLOON TENNIS

For a loony balloon game, see A Balloon, a Spoon, and You.* The clothesline instead of the string will serve as the "net."

WASHDAY RACE

This can be played by a number of children, divided evenly into two teams.

YOU WILL NEED (for each player or each team):

A bucket or basketful of clothes
Clothesline
A handful of clothespins

HERE'S HOW: Each bucket or basket should contain an equal number of pieces of wearing apparel. The first member of each team runs, with the bucket or basket, to the clothesline. He puts down the container and clips all the clothes to the line, one piece at a time. He then runs back to his group and touches off the second member of his team. The teammate runs to the line, takes the clothes off the line, one at a time, and throws them back into the basket. He then runs and touches off the next team member, and this "off and on" routine is repeated until everyone on the team has had a chance. The team that finishes first is the winner.

Here are some beautifully basic back-yard games. Each is a homespun version of a familiar sport.

SPUD GOLF

YOU WILL NEED:

A small cane, umbrella, or stick (with a hook at one end)
A potato

HERE'S HOW: Find a spot in the back yard where there is no grass, just soil. With a stick, draw three circles, one inside another (the small circle should be roughly the size of a saucer, the next circle, surrounding the inner circle, should be about dinner-plate size, and the biggest—outer—circle, as large as you wish).

Write in the dirt (with the point of a stick) the number "20" in the middle of the little circle; "15" in the medium-sized circle, and "5" in the outside circle.

Stand five or six-feet away from this bull's-eye, and putt the potato with the hooked part of the cane, umbrella, or stick. The potato will roll toward the target, and you score according to where the potato stops in the circle. If it lands on the line, no score. The first player to accumulate seventy-five points wins! If you have a paved driveway, you can draw the bull's-eye in chalk and play as described above.

CAN GOLF

If you have a casual, unplanted back yard, this Can Golf can be a source of real family fun.

75

YOU WILL NEED:

A can opener
Small tin cans (clean)
A small shovel (or a large tablespoon)
Marbles, pebbles, golf balls, or Ping-pong balls
Teaspoon, small stick, or pencil (optional)
Small cane, hooked stick, or small umbrella handle (optional)
Ice-cream sticks
White cards
Paste or cellophane tape
Pencil

HERE'S HOW: Remove both ends from a number of clean tin cans (make sure the can opener leaves no sharp edges). Dig small holes in the back yard, about four feet apart. The holes should be just large enough to accommodate the tin cans. (If you dig too wide a hole, insert the can and surround it with dirt, until it is held tightly in the hole.) The open bottom of the can will allow for the drainage of rain water.

Tiny cans (individual-size juice cans or small mushroom cans) are fine if you intend to play with marbles or pebbles; use larger cans for bigger balls. Place the holes (and the cans) in any order you wish, and this pattern will be your "course." The marbles or pebbles can either be flicked between your fingers or hit with a teaspoon, small stick, or pencil. The aim, of course, is to get them into the holes, one after another, right around the "course." The balls can be struck with a small cane, hooked stick, or the handle of a small umbrella.

Stick an ice-cream stick into the ground at each "cup" (hole) and attach (paste or tape) a card showing the number of points that specific hole is worth.

PAPER-CUP POOL

I once played this game on television, and during the entire hour of rehearsal I didn't get a "ball" into a "pocket" once. Then we went on the air, and I pocketed a ball on my first try! I love this game, and I hope you will too.

YOU WILL NEED:

Cellophane or adhesive tape
8 paper cups

A table (an outdoor picnic table is perfect: so is a bridge table)

A handful of tiny balls (either crumpled balls of paper, pebbles, buttons, soda-bottle caps, or beans)

HERE'S HOW: Tape two paper cups to each side of the table, using cellophane or adhesive tape. On the table, place a number of buttons, bottle caps, balls of paper, or large beans. The point of the game is to flick the objects, one at a time, into the cups. If more than one child is participating, each should have a different object with which to play. If one child's "men" are buttons, the other youngster's "men" might be bottle caps.

PARTY PLAY

Give your summer party out in the yard, and it will be a lovely day (if it doesn't rain)! See Party Games.* Also, see the back-yard games described earlier in this chapter.

Here are a couple of games that are just too messy for indoor play, but absolutely right for the great outdoors.

PAINT THE TAIL ON THE BUNNY

The lollipop set likes a new slant on an old game, and instead of "pinning the tail on the donkey," try painting cotton-tails on a big bunny.

YOU WILL NEED:
Lots of stiff soap "paint"
Blindfolds (1 for each child)
Paintbrushes (1 for each child)
Large sheet brown wrapping paper
Crayon
Thumbtacks

HERE'S HOW: Mix a huge bowlful of stiff soap "paint," then blindfold your young guests, one at a time, and arm them with a paintbrush and a small bowl of the suds. Stand each in front of a rabbit drawn on a large sheet of brown wrapping paper and attached to the garage door or to a fence. Let each blindfolded child attempt to paint a blob of a tail on the painting of the bunny. The hostess, standing next to the picture with a crayon, should initial each tail, so that there is no dispute about who "hit the spot."

BOBBING BALLOONS

Balloons are always welcome at a party.

YOU WILL NEED:
Inflated balloons
String
Water-color brushes
Bowls of beaten suds

HERE'S HOW: Blow up a bunch of the balloons and tie them securely in a row, within easy reach of the youngsters. (Either attach them to the top of a fence, or dangle them from the clothesline.) Then hand out water-color brushes in bowls of beaten suds, and have a contest to see who can paint the funniest face on the bobbing globes. The stiffer the soap "paint," the easier it is to make beards and bushy eyebrows. Just use an egg beater (or electric mixer) to whip up the froth. The more soap or detergent you use in proportion to the water, the thicker the consistency.

ANKLES AWAY

This is a very popular game, but I find it too rough for living-room play.

YOU WILL NEED:
    Inflated balloons
    String
    Portable radio (optional)

HERE'S HOW: On each boy's right leg, a balloon is tied (with string) to the outside of the ankle. Then the boys take partners (girls, if you please), and they dance. Of course, you can whistle or hum, but I find that a portable radio is a great help at this point. The aim of the game is to step on (and break) the balloons on all the other boys' ankles, without allowing your own balloon to be broken. The girls try to protect their partners and prevent anyone from stepping on their balloons. The winning couples are those who, at the end of, say, three minutes, have unbroken balloons.

A TASTY SUGGESTION

YOU WILL NEED:
    Glasses
    Soda or lemonade
    Cocktail swizzle sticks or stirrers
    Strawberries, pineapple chunks, pieces of orange, lemons,
        and cherries

HERE'S HOW: For this "summer party special" spear on each stirrer one piece of all the fruit. Then pop one of these "soda kebabs" into each drink and listen to the "oohs" and "ahs."

PICNICS

Confucius says, "The day begins the night before," and this is particularly true when the "day" is a picnic day. Nothing dulls the fun of a picnic as much as the early-morning struggle to prepare the food; the later disappointment of warm, soggy sandwiches and weak, watery lemonade; not knowing what to do when you *get* to the picnic. Don't let anything spoil *your* fun.

HERE'S HOW: *The night before:* Make all the sandwiches, wrap them in silver foil, and place them in the freezer. Mix the lemonade. Put some in your vacuum bottle, and the rest in the ice-cube tray.

In the morning: Take the sandwiches out of the freezer and put them in the picnic bag. Instead of putting plain ice cubes into the lemonade, add the lemonade ice cubes.

When you are ready for lunch, you will find that the sandwiches are no longer frozen, but still fresh and cold. The ice-cold lemonade will not be waterlogged, for as the lemonade ice cubes melt, they turn into more lemonade.

Lighting your barbecue fire needn't be a problem. Find a few waxed cartons (from milk, cream, or orange drinks), split them lengthwise, and place them in the grill (with the openings on top). Fill them with charcoal and light with a match. The burning carton will ignite the coal, and you'll need very little kindling.

If you're going on a picnic with friends, plan an extra surprise for yourselves. Have everyone bring lunch, and then swap lunch bags. You might find something you love, and if not, you can always keep swapping until you do!

COOLIE HAT

After lunch, when the noonday sun beats down on you, make this.

YOU WILL NEED:
 A sturdy paper bag or a large stiff Manila envelope
 Scissors
 Pencil
 Band-Aid
 String

HERE'S HOW: Cut the sides of the paper bag and flatten it out. Draw a circle about fifteen inches in diameter (it need not be perfect) on the paper. Cut or tear it out. Now slit the circle from the edge to the center, and overlap the two edges of the slit. Fasten in this position with a Band-Aid. Tie a knot at the end of a piece of string about a foot and a half in length. Make a tiny hole near the rim of the hat and insert the string near the hole, to be gripped into place by the knot. Repeat on the opposite side of the hat. Place it on your head and tie the two strings under your chin. Now, wouldn't you say that's a real cool coolie hat?

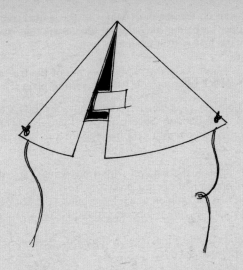

Plan picnic games, and bring along whatever you think you may need (balloons, straws, paper plates, and so forth). See Junior Javelin Throw.* For the paper-plate discus throw you need only one paper plate for each participant. The plates are scaled (thrown so that they sail with the thin edge cutting the air) and the plate that flies the greatest distance wins.

If you are near a stream or brook, see Rubber River Racing,* and Swimming-Pool Sailboats,* which you can make in a second, no matter where you may be.

Around every picnic you will find paper. Use either sheets of newspaper or empty paper bags for this next game.

"THE SIR WALTER RALEIGH HAUL"

YOU WILL NEED:
    2 sheets of newspaper, or 2 paper bags for each couple

HERE'S HOW: Each girl picks a boy, and couples compete against one another. Each couple gets two sheets of newspaper or two paper bags. The girl steps on the first paper (sheet or bag), and the boy, very gallantly, puts the second paper down in front of the girl. She puts her other foot on this second paper, and he lifts the *first* paper, and puts that in front of her, so that she can step on it. In this way, step by step, she progresses from the starting point to the finish mark. She must never step on the ground (ugh!). In this game, only the paper is proper carpeting for her, and the couple that reaches the finish mark first is triumphant.

BALLOON SOCCER

For the boys on a picnic, I recommend a bit of harmless roughhouse, and Balloon Soccer is just that! The balloon moves so slowly, no one can get hurt, and the rules are simply these:

1. Don't touch the balloon with your hands (any other part of the body is just fine)
2. Don't let the balloon touch the ground (the last person to touch it before it hits the ground is "out")

For other balloon games see A Balloon, A Spoon, and You,* and Balloon Tennis.*

CHAPTER IV

Fun Indoors on a Snowy Day

There are few things as infuriating as a blowy, snowy day. It's snow fun (whoops! I mean, it's *no* fun) to stand with your nose pressed against the window, watching all that beautiful snow go to waste!

Well, you can make snowballs, snow men, snow-covered toy houses, snowflakes, or "paint" with colored snow, and still stay snug and safe in the house.

SOAP SNOW

The "snow" is, of course, not real snow—it's made of soap and water, whipped to a froth. For play purposes, this is even better than the real stuff, for soap "snow" won't melt!

YOU WILL NEED:
At least 2 cups packaged soap or detergent
Water
Rotary beater or electric mixer
Bowls
Poster paint or vegetable food coloring
Paintbrush
Pastry tube or cooky press
Spatula

I cannot give you a hard-and-fast formula for whipping up suds, because both the product used and the water found in the particular area can cause variations. In some cases, more soap or detergent will be needed, and in others, more water should be added.

Nevertheless, it is so-oo simple to do.

HERE'S HOW: While the amount of suds needed depends upon the size of the molded piece, start with two cups of packaged soap or detergent and a half cup of water. Whip the mixture with a rotary beater or an electric mixer, adding more soap or water as needed.

For painting, the suds should be loose—a whipped-cream texture. Divide the suds into as many bowls as there are colors to be used. Then add poster paint or food coloring, and apply with a paintbrush.

For making designs with a pastry tube or cooky press, add more soap until the mixture stands in firm, meringue-like peaks. This way it is thick enough to hold the design until it dries, yet thin enough to be worked through openings in the "tools."

For "buttering" suds with a spatula on surfaces such as rooftops, snow-covered lawns, frosted letters, the collars of chimneys, etc., this same meringue-like mixture is excellent.

For molding designs (such as snowballs and snow men), whip in more soap until the mixture resembles dough—if it is difficult to turn a rotary beater, just stir in more soap for a good thick "batter." Then, before picking up the suds to hand mold, dip your hands into water. This will keep the doughy suds from sticking to your hands while you work, and should be repeated as often as necessary.

As this man-made snow dries, it stiffens to a porous texture and lasts for weeks. Not only is it inexpensive to use lavishly, but it creates no mess. What could be easier to clean up than soap?

MOLDING A SNOW MAN

YOU WILL NEED:
    "Soapsuds"
    Candies or buttons
    Piece of cloth
    Black construction paper
    Scissors
    Cellophane tape or rubber cement

HERE'S HOW: Simply prepare a batter thick enough for snowballs. Keep packing until you have enough for a large ball, a medium-sized one, and a small one. Pile one on top of another to form a typical snow man. Use candies or buttons to indicate eyes, nose, and mouth. Twist

84

a piece of cloth around the "neck" of the snow man, for a scarf. On his head, put a black construction paper Hi-Hat.

To make a Hi-Hat, cut a strip and a ring of black construction paper. Bend the strip until it forms a tube, and tape the edges so that it remains in this circular position (see illustration). Then put the tube over the ring, and either tape or rubber-cement it in place. Plop the black Hi-Hat on the top of your snow man while the "snow" is still damp, and it will stick permanently to his head.

THE SOAPSUDS HOUSE

YOU WILL NEED:

A cardboard grocery carton
A laundry shirt cardboard
Cellophane tape
"Soapsuds"
Vegetable food coloring
Black wool or string
A long paper tube or box (optional)
Paper clip
A big board or covered tabletop
Gumdrops

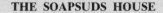

HERE'S HOW: Start with a small grocery carton, and add a pointed roof, made of the side of another carton (or a laundry shirt cardboard). Tape the pointed roof to the "house" carton. Coat the cardboard carton with suds. Use white suds for the body of the house and add food coloring to some of the suds, for a colored roof. Outline drains, doors, and windows with black yarn. If you wish, make a chimney for the side of the house from a long paper-cup carton or a cardboard tube from paper toweling. Attach the chimney to the house with cellophane tape, and use a twisted paper clip for a TV antenna, taped on top of the chimney.

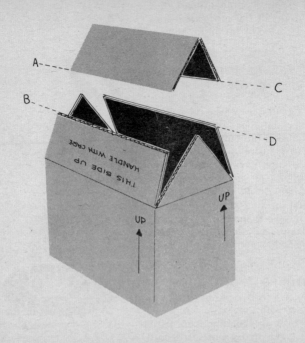

Place your house on a big board (or on a bridge table, covered with a plastic cloth or oilcloth). Cover the cloth or board with suds "snow" too, and, with the black wool or yarn, make a path running from the front of the house through the yard. Place trees and gumdrop "stones" on your snow-covered front lawn.

SNOWBALLS

See Soap Snowballs* for directions.

SNOW "PAINTING"

See Window Painting* and Magic Painting* for various ways to paint with colored snow suds. Here is a dry-paint method.

YOU WILL NEED:
  Brown wrapping paper
  Paintbrush
  Glue
  Packaged soap or detergent
  Basin or bowl

HERE'S HOW: Draw or trace any outline that you wish (a cat, a face, or even a landscape) on the wrapping paper with a brush dipped in glue. Then shake packaged soap or detergent onto the masterpiece. The picture can be upended so that the excess "sparkle" falls into a waiting basin or bowl. What remains is stuck firmly onto the lines of glue, making a fascinating raised design.

All real snowflakes have two things in common—they have exactly six points, and they last only a moment. In all other respects, they differ. Each snowflake has a different program, a distinctive design, a special lovely lacy structure of its own.

SNOWFLAKES

Make pretty paper snowflakes of tissue paper (to fasten to the window), of napkin paper (to attach to dark construction paper, for greeting cards), or of paper, shellac, and glitter (to stiffen and hang from light fixtures or on Christmas trees).

YOU WILL NEED:
    White paper (whatever type is available)
    Pencil
    Cups, saucers, soup bowls, or dinner plates
    Scissors (pinking shears produce a lacy effect)

    Additional, optional items:
    Rubber cement
    Confectioners' sugar
    Water
    Dark construction paper
    Shellac
    Glitter (or sequins)
    Thread

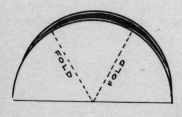
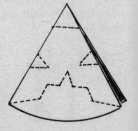

HERE'S HOW: Cut paper circles of different sizes (trace the outline of cups, saucers, soup bowls, and dinner plates). Fold each circle in half. Find the center point along the fold, and then fold these semicircles in thirds. Since a snowflake always has six points, the design should start right in the very corners of the folded paper, and dip down in angles away from the corners toward the center (see illustration).

Snowflakes are always original, so don't repeat or duplicate my design or your own. After cutting each paper snowflake, open it carefully.

Then, either attach it to the windowpane—with a tiny dab of rubber cement, or a paste of confectioners' sugar and water —or mount it on dark construction paper, to be admired, or sent as part of a greeting card; or paint one side with shellac. Before the shellac dries, sprinkle the snowflake with glitter or sequins. Allow it to dry, turn it over, and shellac and sprinkle the other side. The snowflake will stiffen and can be hung by a loop of thread wherever you wish.

FEAST FOR BIRDS

Spend these snowbound hours preparing a feast for hungry little birds. Foraging for food is quite a problem for them when the ground is covered with snow, and you can help.

Popcorn, cranberries, chunks of apple or peanuts
Fat (from last night's dinner meat)
Paper cup
Needle and thread
Teaspoonful of peanut butter
Teaspoonful of crumbs
Old compact with mirror
Bird seed
Pipe cleaner or string

HERE'S HOW: Make chains of popcorn, cranberries, chunks of apple, or peanuts (see Christmas Chains*).

Fat Cups. Birds love fat. Put the pieces in a paper cup (cut the sides down, so that the cup is shallow). Thread a needle and stick it through both sides of the cup. Make a loop and tie a knot. When the snowflakes stop falling, you can hang the little paper bucket on a bush or on the lowest branch of a tree.

Peanut-Butter Cups. Mix a teaspoonful of peanut butter with an equal amount of crumbs and put this in the little paper bucket.

Feeding Tray. Incidentally, the family canary or parakeet will enjoy a little attention too. An excellent toy and feeding tray can be made of an old compact with a mirror in it.

Thoroughly clean the powder compartment and fill the bottom with bird seed. Fasten this feeder to the bars of the cage by tying a pipe cleaner or a piece of string around the hinge of the compact and then twisting the pipe cleaner or piece of string securely around the bars. Birds love to look at themselves in mirrors, and now your bird can enjoy looking and talking to himself as he dines!

Unless I miss my bet, the problems you'll encounter on a snowy day are similar to those you'll find on a rainy day. Please see Chapter I for additional active games.

You'll find that these little suggestions will snowball into hours of snowy-day indoor play, once you get the drift of it!

CHAPTER V

Fun Before the Holidays

GIFT WRAPPING

Wrapping Christmas presents, like any other job, is what you make it. Here are some suggestions that will make it fun!

Let Santa deliver your presents—in person. There are so many ways to turn your package into a Santa Claus. See Chapter VI for dozens of Santa Claus suggestions that can be applied to gift wrapping.

Here's one easy way, which will give you an idea of what I mean.

SANTA PACKAGE

YOU WILL NEED:
> Gift box
> Crepe paper (2 colors) or gift-wrapping paper
> Scissors
> Rubber cement, glue, or paste
> Cellophane tape
> Excelsior (that raffia-like paper that comes as protection
>   with breakable gifts) or cotton
> 2 stamps (Christmas seals) or gummed silver stars
> Construction paper

HERE'S HOW: Cover the box with crepe paper or gift-wrapping paper of any solid color. Cut another strip of crepe paper, of a contrasting color, long enough to wrap around the entire box. This is to be the hat, so rubber-cement this strip of paper around the top edge of the box, with most of the paper sticking up, above the box. Gather the top loose edges of this strip of paper and tape them together, so that the hat comes to a point. A ball of excelsior or a ball of cotton, rubber-cemented to the point, will complete Santa's hat. Rubber-cement more excelsior all around the edges of one side of the box. The row of excelsior at the top will become his hair; on the sides, his sideburns; and on the bottom, his beard. For a truly shaggy Santa, make the excelsior or cotton a bit heavier on the bottom.

Stick two stamps (or stars) onto this side of the box—for eyes—and cut a round nose and a half-moon mouth out of construction paper. Rubber-cement them in the appropriate places, and add the final excelsior or cotton touch—the mustache! Anyone who can rip this package open is heartless —utterly heartless!

Here's a funny gift wrap that could be either a **SANTA POP-UP** or **CLOWN JACK-IN-THE-BOX**

YOU WILL NEED:
  Big gift box
  Red or green paper (gift-wrapping or crepe)
  1 small empty matchbox
  White crepe paper, or construction paper
  Rubber cement
  1 Ping-pong ball or a white poker chip or checker

Black ink or paint
2 thin strips of paper
Scissors
Cotton (optional)

HERE'S HOW: With gift-wrapping or crepe paper, cover the entire gift box and then place it flat on the table. Wrap the matchbox in white crepe or construction paper and cement the covered matchbox to the lower left-hand corner (as it faces you), of the big box. On the white Ping-pong ball, poker chip, or checker, paint a face with ink or paints. Rubber-cement this face in the upper right-hand corner of the box, diagonally across from the matchbox. Paste a little cone of paper on top of the ball, to form the hat.

The "spring" of the Jack-in-the-Box, which connects the head to the little matchbox, is made of two long strips of paper. Lay the ends of the two strips so that they meet and overlap at a ninety-degree angle. Then fold them across each other, always placing the strip that is on the bottom across the one that is on top. Repeat this crossing and folding process until your "spring" stretches from the head to the matchbox. A thin single strip of paper, accordion-pleated and then partly opened, can be substituted for the *double*-strip spring described above.

Rubber-cement the "spring" strip in position (see illustration). Cut two tiny construction-paper hands, cement them on either side of the "spring," and your Jack-in-the-Box is finished!

If you wish him to be a "Santa-in-the-Box," just add bits of cotton for a hat pompon, hatband, mustache, and beard (see Santas* for pictures of similar Santa Clauses).

REINDEER BOX

Speed your gift on its way by putting a reindeer on the wrapping.

HERE'S HOW: Wrap the box. Put two strips of plastic or adhesive tape around the box, one near the very top, the other close to the bottom. With a pencil, draw an angular reindeer with a simple triangular face and straight legs (bent at an angle but not curved). The body should curve gently and should be exactly as wide as the height of the cotton swabs (use a swab as a measure, as you draw).

Then go over your pencil lines with the rubber-cement brush. Lay the swab sticks right into the cement. The antlers, face, and legs are made of pieces of the cotton swabs broken to the correct size. The body consists of a neat row of swabs placed next to one another.

This is one of my favorite gift wraps, and it always breaks my heart when I have to give away a package decorated with this design.

94

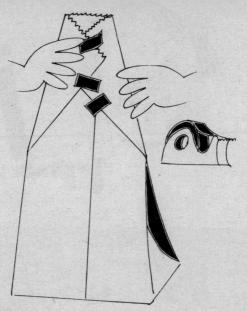

REINDEER BAG

When you give an awkward-shaped gift (such as a mechanical toy), put it in a clean brown paper bag and turn the bag into a reindeer.

YOU WILL NEED:
- Clean brown paper bag
- Cellophane tape
- Scissors
- Cotton or white paper
- Rubber cement
- Cotton swabs
- Gummed silver stars or large sequins
- Tiny Christmas balls or jingle bells

HERE'S HOW: Place the gift in the bag, and fold back the top of the bag. Fasten it in this position with tape. Cut out of cotton or white paper a triangular piece for the head, and two other pieces for the legs (see illustration). Rubber-cement these pieces to the bag. Attach cotton swabs to the headpiece to form antlers. To each leg piece, add a single cotton-swab foot.

Stick or paste on two stars or sequins for eyes, and a round sequin, tiny ball, or jingle bell for the nose. Sprinkle gummed stars and sequins all over the reindeer, and he's ready for the big trip.

SNOW DRIFT

YOU WILL NEED:
　　Soap Snow*
　　Paintbrush or pastry tube
　　Thick or metallic wrapping or brown paper
　　Crayon
　　Chocolate chips, raisins, bits of construction paper, or
　　　　gummed stars

HERE'S HOW: To drift your presents with snow, whip soap flakes or detergent with a bit of water (see Soap Snow* for directions).

Then: *either* dip your paintbrush into the "snow" and write the name of the person who is to receive the gift, or write your season's greetings in "snow" on the box. *Or* press the thick

suds through a pastry tube and make flowers and rosettes. For "Do Not Open Before Christmas" packages, squirt this thick "batter" onto the box top in the form of a big question mark. *Or* draw a small soapsuds snow man on the package— use chocolate chips, raisins, bits of construction paper, or gummed stars for the features.

These soap suggestions work best on thick (or metallic) wrapping or brown paper—not tissue paper.

COTTON BALLS

These can be used to build dimensional designs on your boxes too.

YOU WILL NEED:
    Gift box
    2 cotton balls
    Construction paper
    Scissors
    Paper hat
    Rubber cement

HERE'S HOW: Two balls, one on top of the other, need only two long paper ears to become a rabbit. The same two balls, in that very same position, need only features and a paper hat to turn into a snow man. You can easily attach the cotton to the wrapping paper on the box with rubber cement.

PAPER-RING TREE

Why not put a paper tree on the gift box that is destined to end up under the Christmas tree?

YOU WILL NEED:
    Gift box
    Gummed paper rings
    Gummed stars

HERE'S HOW: Form a tree out of notebook-paper reinforcements (gummed paper rings). Make the trunk three rings wide, four rings high. Then make the lowest branches of the tree eight or nine rings wide, and build up your tree so that each branch has two rings less than the branch below. The very top of the tree (a single ring) should be crowned with a gummed star.

PLASTIC-TAPE TREE

Here's another way to build a Christmas tree onto your Christmas box.

YOU WILL NEED:
    Strips of plastic tape (solid or patterned)
    Scissors

HERE'S HOW: Use a tiny piece of tape at the top, and let the branches (and the strips of tape) get wider and wider. The trunk should be two tapes wide (see illustration). See Christmas Party Invitations* for a typewritten variation on this idea.

TEDDY-BEAR BOX

YOU WILL NEED:
- Gift box
- Brown wrapping or crepe paper
- Cellophane tape
- Scissors
- Brown construction paper
- Laundry shirt cardboard
- Paper ring reinforcements or colored plastic tape
- Double-faced tape or rubber cement
- Ribbon bow
- Brick (optional)

HERE'S HOW: Wrap the box in brown paper and hold wrapping in place with cellophane tape. Cut head, feet, and hands out of brown construction paper, and reinforce the head with cardboard. Tape the head, hands, and feet to the box. Make Teddy Bear's features with colored plastic tape, construction paper, or paper-ring reinforcements. To hold his hands together, place double-faced tape or a dab of rubber cement inside the paws and then press them together. Finish the package with a pink or blue ribbon bow. He can also be used as a book end, if you make him with a brick inside (see illustration).

100

TEE-HEE THE CLOWN

There's no such thing as an indifferent clown. Some are very happy. Others are absolutely miserable. But since gift-giving time is always a happy time, our clown's smile is as broad as the box on which he is made.

YOU WILL NEED:
   Oblong box
   Construction paper (of various colors)
   Scissors
   Red plastic tape or red construction paper
   Rubber cement

HERE'S HOW: Cover two thirds of the box with yellow construction paper. Cover the remaining third of the box with pink construction paper. With a strip of red tape (or a thin strip of red construction paper), cover the line where the pink and yellow papers meet. Your clown now has a red belt.

Let's give him striped pants! Attach long strips of red tape or construction paper, starting at the belt line in the front, continuing around the bottom of the box, and ending at the belt line in the back. Cut, from construction paper or plastic tape, eyes (and eyeballs, please!), a red nose, and that broad grinning mouth we were talking about before. As a final touch, rubber-cement the features on the pink "face" part of the box. You'll find the "face" part *above* the belt line, I trust. If not, start again, because you've obviously made a mistake somewhere.

ELEPHANT BOX

The personal touch! That's all that's needed to turn a simple gift into a treasure. And the pleasure of making an elephant out of a plain box will make you happy too.

YOU WILL NEED:
   A small square box
   Colored wrapping paper or crepe paper
   Cellophane tape
   Scissors
   Black construction paper
   Rubber cement
   Pencil
   ½ yard of ribbon and a bow of the same ribbon

HERE'S HOW: Wrap the box carefully with colored paper. Make sure the loose ends are folded and taped in place on the sides of the box—neatness counts! Cut a long trunk, little eyes, and huge floppy ears out of the construction paper. With rubber cement, fasten the eyes onto the box by putting rubber cement only along the edge of the ears and on the top end of the trunk. Bend both the trunk and the ears so that they stand away from the package. Roll the unattached part of the trunk around a pencil. When you remove the pencil, your baby elephant will have a cute upturned trunk. Now wrap the ribbon around his middle and tape the bow in place on the very top of the box.

An elephant with an upturned trunk is a sign of success, and I'm sure you'll have great success with this one.

MAILING TIPS

Here are some mailing tips that will help your gift packages to arrive in the same shape as that in which you sent them.

To tie a box securely, wet the cord before you tie it. The string will shrink as it dries, which will cause it to fit snugly around the box.

When addressing packages in ink, let the ink dry and then paint over the lettering with colorless nail polish. If the package gets wet, the ink will not blur. Transparent cellophane tape stuck over the lettering will serve the same purpose.

To lick the stamp situation, spare your tongue! Use either a cut potato, a slightly damp kitchen sponge, or an ice cube wrapped in a washcloth to dampen your postage stamps and envelopes.

P.S. A note from your postman: Mail all Christmas packages early!

GREETING CARDS

When you send a greeting card you are supposed to be extending your personal greetings. Make them personal by making them yourself. Use the suggestions in this chapter for no other purpose than to spark your own imagination. After all, if you copy my cards, what you'll really be doing is sending *my* personal greetings to *your* personal friends, and I've never even *met* your friends!

JIGSAW SALUTATIONS

YOU WILL NEED:
  Scissors
  Construction paper
  Envelopes (as large as possible)
  Crayons or paints
  Rubber cement
  Laundry shirt cardboard

HERE'S HOW: Cut the construction paper so that it fits in the envelope without folding. Now draw your greetings and Christmas decorations on one side of the paper. When you are pleased with the design on your construction-paper greeting card, rubber-cement it to the cardboard. Trim the cardboard so that it is the same size as the picture pasted upon it. Now cut the picture (and the board, of course) into about a dozen separate pieces. Cut jagged or curved lines, so that your greeting card really becomes a jigsaw puzzle.

Then address the envelope, drop in all the pieces of the puzzle, and mail.

SEWING SALUTATIONS

This is a "little girls' special." I learned to sew by making these cards—and I loved every minute of it! These can be made two ways, either by an adult, for a little girl to receive and then finish, or by a junior miss, to be sent, completed, to anyone at all.

YOU WILL NEED:
  Pencil
  Small piece of white paper, oak tag, or thin cardboard
  Large darning or tapestry needle
  Colored embroidery threat, yarn, or wool
  Glue or colorless nail polish (optional)
  Paste
  Construction paper (of a Christmasy color)
  Scissors

HERE'S HOW: Draw (or trace from a coloring book or magazine) a picture on the white paper or cardboard. Make it an object with a simple outline, such as a Christmas tree, snow man, butterfly, bird, or flower. Make dots at intervals all around the outline of the picture (make the dots closer together around the curves) and then, with the needle, punch a hole at each dot. Thread the thick yarn, wool, or embroidery thread through the needle, and sew from dot to dot with running stitches, going in and out of the holes, all around the outline. If you prefer, your stitches can fill in the picture, rather than outlining it.

If you are sending this to a young lady who is sick in bed, prepare the thread so that she can sew without a needle. Dip the end of the yarn, wool, or thread into glue or colorless nail polish, roll it to a point, and let it dry.

To make a colorful envelope, paste the picture in the very center of a sheet of construction paper. Cut the sheet of construction paper so that it has four flaps. Then fold the four flaps over the drawing and glue down the top flap. Write the address on the reverse side, and mail.

STICKY SALUTATIONS

This kind of card has a textured quality that I like. It not only looks nice, but it feels nice.

YOU WILL NEED:
    Pencil
    Construction paper, folded in quarters like a greeting card
    Rubber cement (with a brush)
    Soap flakes (or instant coffee, bird seed, absorbent cotton, confetti, glitter, or those tiny multicolored dots of candy used for cake decorations)
    Glue

HERE'S HOW: Draw your greetings, designs, and pictures on the card. Then carefully go over whatever you have drawn with rubber cement (stay within the outline of your lettering or drawing). If you sprinkle the soap flakes all over the card, the flakes will adhere to just the cemented areas, and the drawings (and greetings) will be covered with "snow." If you use bird seed, the effect will be quite different. Try pulling apart absorbent cotton, until it is a rather thin, fluffy film, and laying bits of the fluff into the cement.

Another way of utilizing this technique is to rub the edges of the card with glue and then dip them into gold or silver glitter.

This glue "painting" can be used to good advantage in decorating gift packages too.

Let your greeting cards be representative of you—neighborly (if you're the friendly type), elegant (if you're a sophisticate), or funny (if you're a card)!

CHAPTER VI

Fun at Christmas

Every year, before we've even digested our Thanksgiving turkey dinner, we begin to hear the first faint strains of "Santa Claus Is Coming to Town," and by the time the wishbone has been picked clean, Santa has arrived and is smiling at us from store windows all over America.

The commercial Yuletide uproar is so loud and lasts so long, it's hard to remember that Christmas provides us potentially with more than just a reason for a big buying season. The holiday can be the basis for the kind of fun that you cannot buy—you have to do it yourself.

For many years, I did a daily hour-long TV show on NBC-TV. Six mornings a week, for the entire month before Christmas, I'd show mothers and youngsters of all ages novel and easy Christmasy ways to decorate the house, the tree, the party table, and how to prepare foods and games that were festive and fun.

Here are some of those Christmas ideas, taken from my TV file.

SANTAS

Let's start with Santa Claus, because Santa's smiling face can be used on the tree, at the door, on the party table, in the games—and he can even pop up in the food! Remember, he needs only a white beard and mustache, a red hat, and a round nose to be unmistakably Santa Claus. No matter how poor an artist you think you are, you can make a recognizable, roly-poly Santa. If your house can use a bit more holiday cheer, I bet Saint Nick will do the trick!

SANTA PUPPET

This is an amusing puppet with a moving mouth. A num-

ber of these Santas, hung as tree ornaments, will delight and
entertain all the youngsters who come to see your tree.

HERE'S HOW: Cover the entire box with white paper, but make
sure that the flip-top lid can still open and close. Stand the
box upright on a table, with the flip-top opening on the bottom,
facing you. To make Santa's hat, cut a strip of red crepe
paper (approximately five by ten inches). Apply a band of
rubber cement along the edge of one of the ten-inch sides of
the paper. Then wrap this sticky edge of the paper around
what is now the very top of the box. Most of the crepe paper
will be standing up *above* the box. Carefully gather the top of
the crepe paper together, and, with a small piece of red thread,
tie the paper in this position so that the hat comes to a point.
Now cover the point of the hat with a ball of cotton. Next,
conceal the spot where the hat is attached to the box with a
band of cotton, rubber-cemented in place. Under this "furry"
hatband, glue a pair of small cotton eyebrows. Beneath the
eyebrows, fasten two gummed stars. (Yes, this Santa will have
stars in his eyes.) A Christmas seal or small red circle will
provide him with a nose. The flip-top lid is his mouth, so
around the opening, rubber-cement a cotton mustache and
beard. If you wish, add a wispy fringe of cotton hair (on the
sides of the box, and extending around the back). To attach
the puppet to your tree, make a hole in the back of the box
by pressing the point of a pencil through the cardboard. Then
insert a firm (not droopy) branch of the tree.
    To make his mouth move, hold Santa so that your thumb
is at point A, the rest of your fingers at point B (see illustration). You'll find that gentle pressure of your hand will open
and close his mouth. And if he doesn't start talking right away,
don't be disappointed—if you could read his lips, you'd see
that he is wishing you a "Merry Christmas."

This same little Santa can become a candy container for those cellophane-wrapped Christmas hard candies, at the party table or on the tree. Instead of standing the box on the table so that the flip-top lid is on the bottom, place it with the lid on top, and with the opening facing you. Make the hat as indicated above, but wrap the crepe paper around the lid itself. Now when you flip the lid to get the candy, Santa will tip his hat to you!

BALLOON SANTA

Balloons are a symbol of fun, and a balloon Santa Claus dangling on the tree, hanging in the doorway, or sitting in the center of your party table will help create an atmosphere of holiday cheer.

YOU WILL NEED:
  2 round red balloons for each Santa
  String (preferably black)
  Pencil
  Dinner plate

Red paper (construction or crepe)
Scissors
Rubber cement
Tweezers
Black paper (construction or crepe)
Cotton

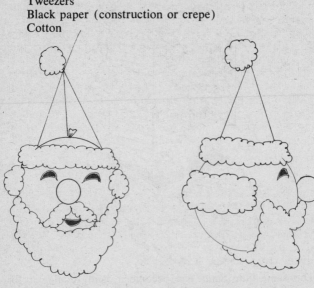

HERE'S HOW: Blow up one of the red balloons as fully as you can. Knot it firmly. Inflate the other balloon just a little, and as soon as it becomes round, knot it. Tie a long black string to the knot on the big balloon. This will make it easy to attach Santa to the tree or doorway. Trace the outline of a dinner plate on the red paper and cut it out. Slit the paper circle to the center, and by overlapping the two edges of the slit, you'll have made a cone-shaped hat. Secure the hat in this position with rubber cement. Apply rubber cement to the inside of the bottom edge of the hat and gently press it, over the knot, onto the big balloon. Make sure the string is loose inside the hat. Cut off about a half inch of the point of the hat, turn the balloon upside down, and shake it until the string appears near the opening at the top of the hat. Then, with the tweezers, pull the loose end of the string through the hole. For Santa's nose, rubber-cement the tiny balloon on the larger one (place it in the middle of the face, with the knot dangling down). The knot will later be covered by Santa's big mustache. Cut three crescent, or half-moon, shapes out of the black paper. Cement two of the crescents above the nose, for eyes.

110

The third, placed about an inch below the nose, will become Santa's mouth. Make a ball of cotton and rubber-cement it onto the hole at the point of his hat. A band of cotton, rubber-cemented to the base of his hat, will become the fur hatband. A slightly wider band of cotton attached to the sides and around the back of his head will give him the traditional fringe of white hair. Two strips of cotton cemented over the knot of the small nose balloon will make a funny mustache. Allow the end of the mustache to droop down. Before you attach the cotton beard, draw the outline of his beard with rubber cement and then fill in the outline with more rubber cement. Don't forget to extend the beard well down under his chin, and up toward his hairline. After you've completed your sticky drawing, place cotton over the entire beard area. That's all. It couldn't be easier, and he couldn't be sweeter.

ONE-PIECE PAPER SANTA

This decorative idea was created and sent to me by a New York kindergarten teacher. Once you have cut out your basic pattern, it's so easy that even the preschoolers in the household will say, "I can do it myself!"

White paper (cut into 6-inch squares)
Crayons (especially red and black)
Scissors
Glue, paste, or rubber cement
Cotton
Yarn or string

HERE'S HOW: At the top of the square, draw a six-inch half circle. Below the half circle, but touching it, draw a complete three-inch circle. The half circle will be the hat; the full circle, the face. Cut along the outline, leaving the hat connected to the face (see illustration). With your crayons, color the hat red (cover the entire half circle) and on the circle itself, draw smiling eyes, a round nose, and a little mouth. "Draw" a mustache (above the mouth) and beard (all over the chin) with glue or cement, and cover the sticky area with cotton. Pull gently on the cotton to shape the beard. Cover the curved edge of the hat (the half circle) with glue or cement and apply a strip of cotton, to give Santa's hat a fuzzy rim. Now bend the straight edge at the top of the hat in half so that it comes to a point and forms a cone. Overlap the two edges, and glue the hat in this position. A tiny ball of cotton glued to the peak of the cone-shaped hat will complete your Santa ornament. You can hang this One-Piece Santa on the tree by means of a loop of yarn run through the top of the hat. These ornaments can be almost mass-produced at home, once you have cut the basic pattern. Make enough paper Santas to dangle all over your tree.

SANTA BABY

When I was a ten-year-old Girl Scout, we all made and wore yarn-doll lapel pins. They were satisfying because we very quickly produced the finished product, and it was so cuddly! Santa Baby yarn dolls are just as simple and appealing.

YOU WILL NEED:
Red wool
2 pieces of cardboard (one 4 inches long,
    the other 4½ inches long)
Scissors
Glue, paste, or rubber cement
3 sequins (or tiny buttons or beads)
Cotton

HERE'S HOW: A) *The Body*. Wind the wool around the four-inch cardboard about sixty times. At the top of the board, slip a single strand of wool (about a foot long) under the wool that is wound around the cardboard. Wrap this strand around the other wool, tie a tight knot, and remove the cardboard. A little below the top knot, tie another tiny piece of wool around the entire hank of wool, to form the neck and the head.

B) *The Arms*. Around the four-and-a-half-inch cardboard, wind more wool (about thirty-five times). Slip two tiny single strands under the wound wool, one at each end of the cardboard, tie them (in two separate knots), and remove the board. Two other tiny wool strands, wound and tied around the hank about a half inch from each end, will form wrists. Place the arms in the middle of the body loop, right under the head. Tie a piece of wool around the waist. Divide the wool below the waist into two even bundles and tie a strand around each bundle, about a quarter of an inch from the bottom. Now Santa has legs and feet. Glue the sequins, buttons, or beads onto the face, so that Santa has two eyes and one mouth. Rubber-cement a bit of cotton on his chin to form the beard. Another dab of cotton, attached over the mouth, will become a mustache. Three tiny balls of cotton parading down his chest will make furry buttons. A fringe of cotton glued around his head (right above his eyes) will become the bottom of his hat. Around the base of the strand of wool at the top of his head, twist and glue a tiny bit of cotton into a ball. Tie this top string into a loop and hang Santa Baby on the tree.

SANTA PLATE PUPPET

I discovered this little fellow during a Christmas party in the children's ward of a New York hospital. He's a decoration, he's a puppet, and he's a real doll!

YOU WILL NEED:
- 2 small paper plates (dessert size)
- 4 large paper plates (dinner size)
- A hole punch (optional)
- String
- Scissors
- Brass paper fasteners
- Red paint and brush
- Black construction paper
- Glue, paste, or rubber cement
- Cotton

HERE'S HOW: Hold the two small paper plates face to face with the bulges (bottoms) on the outside. At the top, punch a hole through the rims of the two paper plates and tie them together. Leave an extra length of string (for hanging). At the bottom, punch another hole through both plate rims. Now place the two large plates face to face and, in the same way, punch a hole at the top. Connect the top holes of the two large plates to the bottom holes of the two smaller ones, leaving about a half inch of slack string between them.

To make legs and arms, cut the rims off one of the two unused large plates and then cut the rim in half. At the bottom, insert these semicircular pieces between the two large plates to form legs. Fasten with paper fasteners. Cut the rim from the last unused large plate and trim this rim into shorter pieces, to serve as arms. Insert the arms between the two large plates (on the sides) and secure these with paper fasteners too. Now paint the body (the large plate) and the arms and legs red. Dab just a bit of red paint on the very top of the small plate, to form the hat. Cut eyes, nose, and mouth out of black construction paper and paste them on the face (the small plate). Cut black paper gloves and boots. When the paint has dried, glue the gloves and boots at the ends of the arms and legs. Attach (with glue) the cotton mustache, beard, buttons, belt, waist, and ankle cuffs, and the hat trim.

SANTA PLATE MARIONETTE

You can turn the Santa Plate Puppet into a marionette.

YOU WILL NEED:
Everything listed above *and* 1 long pencil or ruler

HERE'S HOW: Enlarge all the holes around the paper fasteners so that the arms and legs can move easily. Make holes at the ends of his arms and legs and at the top of his head. Tie strings through these holes and attach them to a long pencil or ruler. Try hanging this Santa on your door, and see if your guests don't enter smiling!

ALL-THROUGH-THE-HOUSE DECORATIONS

Here are some unusual ideas that will make your home bloom with the holiday spirit, whether you have a tree or not.

CHIMNEY CARTON

This mock-brick chimney should be large enough to hold lots of small presents.

YOU WILL NEED:
   A tall cardboard grocery carton
   Brick-patterned paper (crepe, Con-tact, or wallpaper),
      or poster paints and brushes
   Paste
   Poster paints (optional)
   Soap flakes
   Water
   Egg beater (manual or electric)

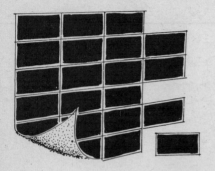

116

HERE'S HOW: The basis for the chimney is a tall cardboard grocery carton with the top flaps removed. Brick-patterned crepe paper, Con-tact paper, or wallpaper pasted around the entire outside of the carton will quickly turn it into a chimney (ten minutes and some poster paints will do just as well). When the glue or paint has dried, add the "snow" topping. The "snow" is made of beaten soap (see Soap Snow* for the simple instructions).

Heap all the presents into the chimney, and place it either under the tree or in the center of the room. Perhaps Santa couldn't manage to squeeze himself down the chimney, but he deposited his happy load, anyway!

WINDOW PAINTING

This kind of Christmas decoration is easy, and inexpensive, and none of these techniques requires that you have a peewee Picasso around the house.

UNTRADITIONAL STAINED-GLASS WINDOWS

YOU WILL NEED:
>   Scouring powder
>   Water
>   Empty glass jars
>   Poster paints (or vegetable food coloring) and brushes
>   Slightly damp, thin piece of cloth

HERE'S HOW: Mix a thick paste of scouring powder and water. Divide the goo between a number of jars and add a bit of poster paint (different colors) to each jar. Be sure to make one jar of black soap-paint mixture. Do not add paint to one big jar of goo, and this will be your white, useful for snow scenes or for white accent. You can substitute food coloring for paint.

The simplest way to window-paint with this mixture is to cover the entire window area, applying the soap mixture with your fingertips. Let it dry. Use whatever color you wish for this basic film. Then wrap a slightly damp, thin piece of cloth over your index finger and outline whatever you wish to draw (trees, angels, houses, snow men, etc.). The basic film of soap will be removed wherever you "draw" with the damp cloth. Next, decide where in your picture you wish color (the tree or the star on top of the tree, the roof, the

118

house, the snow man's hat, etc.). With the clean part of the damp cloth wrapped around your finger, remove the film from that portion of the picture and replace it with whatever color you wish. Leave a thin blank border of no color between your all-over background and your filled-in areas of color. Now dip a paintbrush into the jar of black goo and fill in all the blank borders. This black edging around your pictures will simulate the lead outlining in a real stained-glass window.

For example: on a pane of glass I put a film of light green and outlined a flower. I removed the soap-paint film from inside the outline, and the flower was then filled with light blue mixture. The stem, leaves, and center I painted a darker green (see illustration).

At night, the lights of your home will turn your "picture" window into a warm and wonderful sight, when viewed from the street.

SILHOUETTES IN THE SNOW

Try combining the scouring-powder mixture with paper silhouettes.

YOU WILL NEED:
All the items listed above *and*
Black or colored construction or wrapping paper
Scissors
Cellophane tape or rubber cement

HERE'S HOW: Cover the entire window with the basic soap film. Out of black (or colored) construction or wrapping paper, cut the silhouettes of certain parts of your picture (perhaps the Christmas trees or just the star or angel on top of the tree—or the windows of the house in your picture could be cut out of paper, and the rest of the picture outlined with black paste, as described above, in Untraditional Stained-Glass Windows*). Remove the basic film on the particular section of the picture before applying the silhouette. Attach the silhouettes to the window with tiny bits of cellophane tape or little dots of rubber cement.

GREETINGS IN THE SNOW

The scouring-powder mixture or a mixture of two parts soap flakes and one part water, beaten till stiff, provide the ideal windowpane and mirror writing medium. Christmas

greetings on windowpanes and mirrors make a house look very gay indeed! Just remember to spell the holiday message backward when you are painting on the windowpane, otherwise the words will be seen in reverse by friends as they approach the house.

I decorated my large rehearsal mirror at home (see illustration). I found that the nicest part of this kind of painting is the reassuring fact that you can wipe away your mistakes and start again, and no one will ever know!

After the holidays, wipe the windows and mirrors clean with a damp sponge. The scouring powder or soap flakes in the mixture actually do the cleanup job with very little help from you. Put old rags or paper toweling at the bottom of the window or mirror to soak up the drippings.

SNOW SHAPES AND GLITTERY GREETINGS

These are 3-D Christmas decorations. Your favorite season's greetings, written in dimensional letters, will keep the holiday spirit around for a long time.

1 tablespoon plastic starch
1 cup detergent

Egg beater (manual or electric)
Laundry shirt cardboard (or cereal-box cardboard)
Pencil
Scissors
Confetti (or glitter, sequins, or tiny colored candies)
Black thread
Cord (optional)
Tiny colored plastic clothespins (optional)

HERE'S HOW: First mix a tablespoon of plastic starch with one cup of detergent. Whip it until it reaches the consistency of cake frosting and then let it stand. Next, on cardboard, draw the outline of Christmas trees, stars, or perhaps separate block letters spelling "Merry Christmas" or "Happy New Year" (or any other holiday greeting). Cut out the cardboard shapes. Coat these cutouts on both sides with the detergent-starch mixture. Press them gently on the window glass, and hold them in position against the pane until the mixture hardens and they "set." When the holiday is over, you just have to apply a wet cloth until the hard plastic turns into frothy suds, and then rinse these off.

If you'd like to use this idea on your Christmas tree, cut out cardboard letters spelling "Merry Christmas" (or, if you wish, the names of each child in the household) and coat the letters with the detergent-starch mixture (or "snow" suds, made of two parts soap and one part water, beaten till stiff). While the coating is still wet, sprinkle the letters with confetti, glitter, sequins, or tiny colored candies (the kind used for cooky decoration). When dry, these sparkling letters can be hung on your Christmas tree. Simply attach a black thread loop to the top of each letter and hang on the branches.

One New Year's Eve, I gave a party, and used this idea to brighten up the hall. I stretched a cord across my hallway and attached the letters to the cord with tiny colored plastic clothespins. A good time was had by all!

SOCKS FOR SANTA

Hang these on the fireplace or at the foot of the bed. Home-made felt socks are a cinch to make, a joy to behold, and a pleasure to give (or receive) as a present! No sewing is necessary.

YOU WILL NEED:
Laundry shirt cardboard

Pencil

Scissors (preferably pinking shears)

Felt (at least 3 colors)

Rubber cement

Sequins or flat buttons

Bits of rickrack, fabric, or ribbon

HERE'S HOW: On the cardboard, draw a number of big sock outlines until you arrive at one that you like. Cut it out and trace the outline on the felt. Cut two identical felt sock shapes by cutting through two layers of felt at the same time. Brush a border of rubber cement all around one of the sock shapes. Let it dry slightly, and then press the other sock on top of the sticky one so that they match exactly, heel to heel and toe to toe. For even greater strength, brush the cement around both sock shapes, on the sides that are to go face to face.

This is your basic sock, and shape, size and decorations are up to you. I always make the sock shape rather large (it can hold more goodies that way). The general decorations are all rubber-cemented onto the front of the sock. The sequins and buttons may be placed symmetrically or not, to suit your taste. The rickrack may be rubber-cemented around the entire outline of the sock, or perhaps only in a straight line along the heel-to-toe section. The central design may be any Christmas symbol, cut from felt or fabric, and cemented in place. You might enjoy decorating your sock with a Christmas tree (or a scattering of trees of different sizes), a reindeer (perhaps you can find a magazine picture of a reindeer that you would like to trace), a snow man, or an angel.

I have found that these colorful socks make superb packages in which to wrap little gifts to be left under the tree, and because they are made of materials that last and last, these festive felt socks, packed away after the holiday, can become part of your own Christmas tradition.

BALLOON REINDEER

Twisting balloon animals is usually done by professional entertainers, but it's so easy that anyone can do it. Don't worry about the balloons breaking. If they do, everyone will get a big "bang" out of it! These instructions are for making balloon reindeers only, but other animals are just as simple. By varying the length of the legs, ears (or horns), neck, body, and tail, you can make a dachshund, giraffe, poodle, swan, or even a rabbit. They are easy to create, once you get the knack of the single, basic twist.

YOU WILL NEED:
   4 long straight balloons, inflated (but not to the bursting point) and well knotted

HERE'S HOW: Place both hands about a quarter of the way down the balloon from the knot. They should be next to (and touching) each other, and both gripping the balloon. Twist your hands quickly in opposite directions, and the balloon will divide into two sections, connected between your hands by a thin "neck" (see illustration). Put the balloon under your arm, gripping it between your arm and body. You can hold

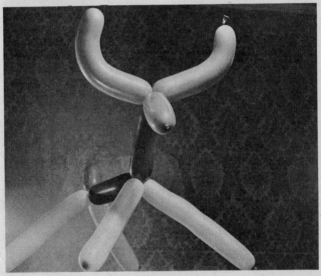

it in this twisted position and still have your hands free. Next, place your hands right in the middle of the second balloon, and twist it in the same way. Hold this second (twisted) point between the thumb and index finger of one hand; and between the thumb and index finger of your other hand, grab the twisted point of the balloon that is under your arm. Hold these two thin "necks" so that they are crossing one another (in this position the balloons will form an X). Wind the top balloon around and under the bottom one, and vice versa (see illustration). If you take your hands away, the two balloons should now be entwined—barring an accident, of course! The shortest section of the balloons has a knot at the end of it, and this will be the reindeer's head. The two long even sections are the antlers. The remaining long piece is the body to which the legs will be attached. Connect two more balloons to this long body section, repeating the entire procedure (as you did to make antlers) twice again, to create the two sets of legs. Of course the legs get twisted so that they reach downward, while the antlers stick up in the air (see illustration). These balloon "Rudolphs" are lovely to make for decorations before the company comes. If your guests are older than, say, nine years of age, they'll enjoy making their own animals and creating original monsters. Just supply them with a large number of good-quality colored rubber balloons, and stand by to help tie the knots.

TREE DECORATIONS

I firmly believe that only God can make a tree. I have never been able to discover a do-it-yourself Christmas tree that could compare with the tiniest real fir tree. On the other hand, this is certainly not true of Christmas-tree ornaments. I don't think there is a store-bought ornament anywhere that will give you the pleasure you can get from simple home-made tree decorations with a personal touch!

Here are easy and effective ways to make Christmas-tree bells, balls, stars, snow, chains, and candy containers. Many of the Santa Clauses described earlier in this chapter would love to perch on your tree.

Don't hesitate to improvise and use your imagination. Your trees should reflect your family's personality.

Here's how some famous people enjoy the holiday:

Sophisticated Betty Furness's tree is bedecked with golden ornaments only, attached with golden bows.

Marlene Dietrich believes that you cannot put too much on a tree, and she hangs so many ornaments and toys, you cannot see the tree itself.

At the home of Herbert Mayes (editor of *McCall's Magazine*) I saw an enormous tree, magnificently decorated with huge, elegant artificial flowers.

Big Bud Palmer (the sportscaster) buys the hugest tree he can find. (He says he always overjudges it, and he has to chop the tree down a bit when he gets it home.) He lets the children choose the decorations and do the actual trimming on the night before Christmas, and whatever his nine-year-old daughter, Betty, makes in school is hung prominently on the tree.

Paul Winchell and his family put all sorts of tiny toys on their tree.

Each of these people considers Christmas the time to have their own special kind of fun with the kids. Why don't you?

SILVER STARS

YOU WILL NEED:
Gummed silver stars
Damp kitchen sponge
Black thread

HERE'S HOW: A box of large silver-paper stars (the kind with gummed backs) and a spool of black thread can make your tree twinkle with star light, star bright. On a tabletop, lay a row of stars face down (with the gummed surfaces toward you). Arrange the stars approximately five inches apart. With a dampened kitchen sponge, moisten each gummed back.

Unroll a length of black thread, but do not cut it from the spool. Lay the thread so that it cuts across the top point of all the stars. Carefully press onto each sticky star the moistened gummed surface of another star, with the two gummed sides facing one another. The two stars will hold the thread securely between them. Be sure that they meet at all five points. Your two stars will now look like one, with shiny surfaces front and back.

Place more stars on the table (in a row, face down, with the gummed side toward you), unroll more thread, and repeat the entire procedure until you have a sufficient number of threaded stars to encircle your tree completely.

SPARKLY SWAB-STICK STARS

These stars are a cinch to make, and even a small child can help prepare them.

YOU WILL NEED:
    A box of cotton swabs (small sticks with
        cotton at each end)
    Paint (ordinary water colors will do, but fluorescent
        paint is even more effective)
    Glue or rubber cement
    Black thread
    Gold glitter

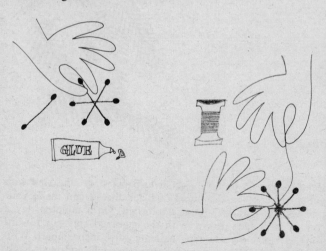

HERE'S HOW: Four swabs are needed for each star. Dip the cotton tips of the sticks in paint and let them dry. Dab a bit of glue or rubber cement in the center of the sticks, and cross them, one on top of another. Then bind them at the center with thread, leaving an extra length of thread for attaching the stars to the tree. Brush glue or rubber cement along the length of the swabs, and sprinkle on glitter. That's all there is to it! These sparkly Christmas stars can be hung on the tree or fastened onto a package, as part of a festive gift wrap.

SODA-STRAW STARS

Colored soda straws (either paper or cellophane) make beautiful star bursts.

YOU WILL NEED:
Scissors
Colored soda straws (paper or cellophane)
Black thread

HERE'S HOW: Cut the straws into even lengths (about two and a half inches each). Fold each length of straw in half to find the center, and flatten that center point between your fingers. With a piece of strong black thread, tie together fifteen soda-straw pieces (see illustration). Then spread out the ends of the straws and hang the star star bursts on the tree.

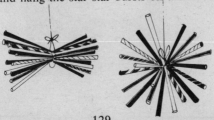

SILVER BELLS

These bells may not ring, but on a "Silent Night" they will brighten up your Christmas tree.

YOU WILL NEED:
   Aluminum foil
   A bell-shaped jelly glass
   Needle and black thread
   Scissors
   Cellophane tape

HERE'S HOW: Silvery bells of aluminum foil can be shaped over an inverted jelly glass. Press the foil over the glass and then gently lift off the bell-shaped silver. Crimp the bottom edge. Crumble a tiny ball of foil for the "clapper." Thread a needle with a one-foot length of black thread, and make a knot at the end of it. Stick the needle through the tiny foil ball and push the ball to the bottom of the thread. It will rest on the knot. Then pierce the top of the silver-foil bell and pull the thread through, until the crumpled ball "clapper" can barely be seen below the lip of the bell. A tiny piece of cellophane tape placed over the needle hole inside the bell will keep the clapper in this position. Use the piece of thread sticking out of the top of the silvery bell to attach it to a branch of your tree. If you prefer, your tree lights can be the "clappers" too. Just punch a hole in the top of the bell to fit around the entire tiny light bulb. When the bell is in position, crimp the edges of the hole at the top, around the bulb, to hold it there.

EGG-CITING EGG-CARTON BELLS

YOU WILL NEED:
>Scissors
>Egg cartons
>Paint or gilt
>Paintbrush
>Tiny silver jingle bell
>Needle and thread
>Aluminum foil (optional)

HERE'S HOW: Cut out the individual, cup-shaped sections of egg cartons, and gild or paint them. Thread a tiny silver jingle bell to serve as the clapper (a ball of crumpled foil will do just as well). Punch a small hole in the top of the bell, and string the clapper in the right place.

POPCORN BALLS

Make glittering and inviting Christmas decorations out of popcorn balls, wrapped in silver foil, tied with bright ribbon, and hung on the tree. They're easy to make, nice to look at, and good to eat. All in all, you'll have a ball! I make these popcorn balls right in the popping pan.

YOU WILL NEED:
>¼ cup corn oil
>½ cup unpopped popcorn
>½ cup corn syrup
>½ cup sugar
>½ teaspoon salt
>Butter
>Vegetable food coloring (optional)
>Silver foil
>Bright ribbons

HERE'S HOW: Heat the corn oil in a large kettle, over medium heat, for three minutes. Add popcorn and cover, but leave a little space for air. Shake frequently, until the popping stops. Mix together corn syrup, sugar and salt, and add this mixture to the popped corn in the kettle. Stir it constantly over a low flame for three to five minutes, until the sugar is dissolved and the corn is completely coated with the syrup mixture. Remove it from the heat and put a little butter on the palms of your hands. Form the popcorn into balls, using as little pressure as possible. If you want colored popcorn balls, tint the corn-syrup mixture with food coloring *before* you add the syrup mixture to the popped corn. When the popcorn balls have cooled and dried, wrap them neatly in silver foil. Tie the balls with bright ribbon and hang them on the tree.

SUGGESTION FOR STORE-BOUGHT ORNAMENTS

The standard commercial Christmas ornaments are lovely but generally not shatter-proof! To keep them from breaking, remove the little hanger (or hook) on top, and pour a bit of white shellac into the opening at the top of the ball. Swish the fluid around for a minute and then pour out the excess. Before you replace the hanger, let the ball stand overnight. The shellac will dry and make your Christmas ornaments much more tree-worthy!

CONE-CUP CANDY CONTAINER

Some people like to have candy on the tree for visiting children to remove and enjoy. The Santa Puppet* (flip-top-box Santa) will hold lots of candy. This Cone-Cup Candy Container will serve as a beautiful tree ornament, but don't put too much candy in it, or you'll find that your cup runneth over!

YOU WILL NEED:
>   Needle and black thread
>   Pointed paper cups
>   Glitter, sequins, or tiny buttons
>   Wax paper
>   Rubber cement
>   Paints and brush (optional)
>   Cake of soap (optional)

HERE'S HOW: Stick a threaded needle through the paper on the side of the cup, about an inch below the lip. Make a loop of thread and tie a knot. Your cup will hang on the tree by this loop. If you are working with glitter, spread it out on a large piece of wax paper. Brush rubber cement over the entire outer surface of the paper cone. Now roll this sticky surface of the cup in the glitter, until it is covered with the sparkly bits. Hang it up by the loop, to dry. If you are using sequins instead of glitter, cover the outside of the cup with rubber

cement, then place the sequins on the rubber cement in any pattern or design you wish. Tiny colorful buttons can be substituted for sequins or glitter.

These cups can also be painted. If the outer surface is waxy, wipe your paintbrush over a cake of soap before dipping it into the paint. This will help the paint adhere to the waxed surface.

When they are decorated, fill these pretty cones (but not to the brim) with cellophane-wrapped hard candies or chocolate kisses.

CHRISTMAS CHAINS

To drape your tree, scour the house for colorful things that can be threaded. Big beads, broken bits of jewelry, or bright buttons might fill the bill. Try popcorn strung on a strong black thread. For a red and white color scheme, popcorn and cranberries can be alternated. After the tree comes down, these chains can be put out-of-doors on branches of bushes and trees, and the birds will enjoy your holiday celebration too!

Straw chains are delicate and easy to make. Just cut colored soda straws into one- or one-and-a-half-inch pieces with tiny nail scissors. Cut six slits in one end of each piece. Press these slits outward, so that on the end of each piece of straw is a tiny star burst. Thread a great many of these, and drape your straw chain around the tree.

"SNOW"

You can provide a white Christmas on your indoor tree, no matter what the weatherman has done to the trees outside. This tree "snow" is guaranteed not to melt, and, more importantly, not to burn (that's my main objection to homemade cotton "snow"). For the basic recipe see Soap Snow.*

YOU WILL NEED:
    Soap Snow*
    String
    Sequins, beads, glitter, or tiny candies
    Plastic cloth or oilcloth

HERE'S HOW: Mold the suds (the consistency should be like stiff meringue) into snowballs, and include in each ball the end of a length of strong string (for hanging). While still slightly damp, they can be sprinkled with sequins, beads, glitter, or tiny candies (the kind used in cooky decoration). These silly snowballs are welcome tree ornaments that literally last for years. Place a plastic cloth or oilcloth around the base of the Christmas tree and surround the tree with a pile of snowballs. Then drift stiffly beaten "snow" suds onto your Christmas-tree branches and pine wreaths. Just scoop up a handful of suds and brush it over the greenery.

CHRISTMAS TABLE DECORATIONS

Christmastime is get-together time, and no matter what form your get-together may take, you'll want it to be as special as the spirit of the season itself.

There are many parts to any party, and if you plan properly, each part will contribute to the sum of the fun. All the decorations and favors I've mentioned in the earlier sections of this chapter may be included in your party. The many Santa Claus suggestions are particularly adaptable for use as table decorations and take-home favors.

Here are some Noel novelties that will cover all the neces-

sary—or, at any rate, recommended—steps in planning and executing a Christmas fun fest.

POPCORN-BALL SNOW MAN

These snow men are tremendously easy and wonderfully decorative, but don't expect your young guests to eat them at the party—they won't! Popcorn-Ball Snow Men always go home, to be admired and *then* devoured!

YOU WILL NEED:
  Popcorn Balls*
  Corn syrup
  Raisins or gumdrops
  Toothpicks
  Flat cooky
  Marshmallow
  White paper (optional)

HERE'S HOW: Make Popcorn Balls.* Then pile two regular-

135

sized popcorn balls one on top of another. Connect them with corn syrup, brushed on top of the lower ball. Place a third popcorn ball (a smaller one) on top of the other two, connecting it in the same way, with the corn syrup. This will be the head. Attach eyes, nose, mouth, and buttons (made of raisins or gumdrops) with dots of corn syrup or bits of toothpick. Stick two whole toothpicks into the sides of the middle ball, to become Mr. Snow Man's arms.

For a funny snow man's hat of black construction paper, see Hi-Hat.* A quick, amusing, and edible hat can be made by brushing corn syrup onto the top of the popcorn snow man's head and placing a flat cooky on the syrup. Then put a dot of corn syrup in the middle of the cooky, and press on a marshmallow, to form the crown of the hat.

Incidentally, these Popcorn-Ball Snow Men make adorable place cards. Simply make small pennants (triangles) out of white paper, and write each guest's name on one of these pennants. Attach a pennant to each snow man by spearing it onto one of the toothpick arms. The snow men will hold the place cards in full view for all to see, and they'll look cute enough to eat.

MARSHMALLOW CHRISTMAS TREE

YOU WILL NEED:
    Marshmallows
    Toothpicks
    Gummed silver or gold stars

HERE'S HOW: Place the first marshmallow flat side down, to serve as the wide trunk of the tree. I suggest that you wet your toothpicks before sticking them into the marshmallows. This makes them easier to insert. Brace a wet toothpick, half in this "trunk" marshmallow and half in another marshmallow, which is standing on its side directly on top of the trunk. Stick three wet toothpicks halfway into the second marshmallow. One should be sticking out on each side, and one on top. In this way, build your marshmallow tree.

I've made the lowest branch of my tree three marshmallows wide. Into the marshmallow at the very top of the tree, stick a toothpick so that just about a half inch protrudes. Paste two small silver or gold gummed stars, back to back, with the sticking sides together, over this piece of the toothpick.

The very tiny marshmallows (available in most grocery stores) are fun too, for building churches or igloos. Try using cubes of sugar for constructing buildings and walls. Layers of corn syrup will hold your "bricks" in place. I hope these ideas are just the building blocks for a world of fun, exploring the possibilities inherent in these unorthodox construction materials.

CHRISTMAS PARTY INVITATIONS

Type your party invitations so that the words form the shape of a Christmas tree. Paste a gummed silver star on top of each tree.

If you type these on thin paper, you can make four or five carbons at a time.

HERE'S HOW:

★

YOU

ARE INVITED

TO A CHRISTMAS

PARTY ON SUNDAY, DECEMBER 22

AT 1 P.M. BRING A GIFT, WHICH WILL BE

GIVEN TO A NEEDY CHILD. THE PARTY WILL BE

HELD AT 20 MAIN STREET AND WILL BE OVER AT 4:30 P.M.

R. S. V. P.

SHARI

LEWIS

MARSHMALLOW STATUES

Marshmallows are as adaptable for table decoration as Building Blocks* are for children's play. They can be piled standing on their sides, or placed flat, one on top of the other.

Experiment with your own marshmallow sculpture. Here are the building plans for constructing a Marshmallow Christmas Tree. You need no instructions for making the Marshmallow Snow Man (see illustration). He's an easy-does-it fat and funny mashmallow fellow!

PIPE-CLEANER REINDEER

These reindeer are the skinniest, most spindle-legged reindeer you've ever seen, but, after all, they only have to travel from your work table to your party table. They make this trip with such ease! A few snips and a couple of twists, and the result is undeniably an underweight but overpoweringly sweet little reindeer.

YOU WILL NEED:
    3 pipe cleaners
    Scissors
    Red bead, needle and thread or red nail polish, paint, or
       crayon

HERE'S HOW: A) *Legs*. Cut one pipe cleaner in half.

            B) *Body and Antlers*. Cut about two inches off each of the remaining two pipe cleaners. The two smaller pieces will be the little antlers. Of the two big pieces left, one

138

will be used for the body and the other for the big antlers.

Bend the body piece so that it has the general contour of a head, a neck, a back, and a tail. Twist the legs around the body, so that the reindeer can stand. Add the big antlers (see illustration for general positioning) and then twist the two small antlers near the ends of the big antlers. A tiny red bead sewn to the tip of his nose will make your reindeer a true "Rudolph." Red nail polish, paint, or crayon will do the job too.

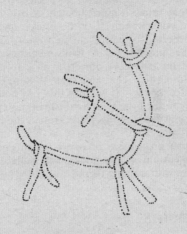

CARTON CANDY CHIMNEY

Make tiny snow-topped brick chimneys to hold wrapped hard Christmas candies. These are amusing and useful on your Christmas table, and they will be cherished as party favors by the youngsters.

YOU WILL NEED:
  Milk or cream containers
  Scissors
  Paints and brush
  Soap flakes or detergent
  Water
  Sandpaper (a couple of large sheets)
  Ruler and pencil

HERE'S HOW: Cut the milk cartons down to whatever size you wish your chimney to be. (Cream containers need to have only the tops removed.) You can paint bricks on the wax container by rubbing your paintbrush over a cake of soap before dipping it into the paint. I think these little brick chimneys are far more fun if you actually cut miniature bricks out of sandpaper and apply them to the sides of the waxed carton with a "mortar" of soap. Mix soap flakes or detergent with a bit of water (make a thick paste). With your fingertips, scoop up the mixture and press it onto the sides of the wax cartons. If you keep a bowl of clear water nearby, a dampened finger will easily level the surface. On the back of a sheet of sandpaper, rule off individual bricks (approximately a half inch by an inch). Cut them out carefully. Lay the bricks, one at a time, into the soap "mortar." Place them in rows, staggering the rows so that the finished "wall" looks realistic. Then frost the top edges of the chimney with drifts of soap mortar, and allow the soap to harden. The same soap mixture can be used for mortar and for "snow." It will dry in a few hours. Fill the finished chimney to the brim with hard Christmas candies, and put one chimney at each child's place around the party table. These candy chimneys can also serve as place cards. Write each guest's name on a piece of paper which you have cut to the same dimensions as the bricks, and replace one brick on each chimney with a name tag.

SNOWBALL LIGHTS

Watch the children's eyes light up at the sight of these snowball lights, placed on your party table or on the mantel. I like these because the snowball will last for years (you replace the tiny candle, which is almost hidden), and the flame cannot be knocked over.

YOU WILL NEED:
>Water
>Soap flakes
>Egg beater (manual or electric)
>A tiny bottle—I use a little medicine (pill) bottle
>Short candle (one that fits into the bottle)

HERE'S HOW: Measure one part of water to two parts of soap flakes. Whip the mixture (with the egg beater) until it is rather stiff. Starting from the bottom, coat the bottle with the soap mixture until it is covered. Keep adding layers until it becomes ball-shaped. Apply the soap with your fingertips, and the snowball will have a rough "snow" texture. Allow the snowball to dry overnight, and then insert a small candle into the bottle. The prettiest illusion occurs when only the flame shows above the ball, and as the candle burns down inside the bottle, you see just a lovely glow.

CHRISTMAS PLACE MATS AND COASTERS

A simple white cloth (even a paper one) can be the basis of a party-table conversation piece. Make place mats and coasters that are practical and pretty.

PINE-TREE PLACE MATS

YOU WILL NEED:
 Pencil
 Large sheet of paper (grocery-bag paper will be fine)
 Scissors (pinking shears are even better)
 Green and red blotter paper (large desk-size sheets)

HERE'S HOW: Draw the outline of a wide-based Christmas tree (approximately sixteen inches high) on the paper, and when you are satisfied with the shape, cut it out and trace your tree pattern onto the green blotter paper. Cut one Pine-Tree Place Mat for each guest. Cut small stars and bells out of red blotter paper, to serve as very efficient (and thirsty) coasters, to put under drinking glasses.

FANCY FELT PLACE MATS

These are elegant and make original gift items. The nicest thing about this idea is that it is a quick cut-and-paste project —no sewing necessary. Set your table with these place mats, and you'll have the perfect setting for a beautiful party.

YOU WILL NEED:
 Pinking shears or scissors
 Felt (any colors you wish)
 Sequins
 Buttons
 Bits of ribbon or rickrack
 Rubber cement

HERE'S HOW: Cut rectangles (perhaps fourteen by nineteen inches) out of the felt. If you use pinking shears, the mats will need no hemming. Now cut decorative felt shapes with which to trim the mats. These shapes can be as fancy or as simple as you wish. Try a single green felt tree on a red mat, or a small circle of red felt, decorated with sequins (to look like a Christmas ornament) on a white mat. This felt "ornament" can look as though it is "hung" on one side of the mat by attaching (above the red circle) a strip of pretty ribbon. The trimmings should be rubber-cemented along the sides and in the corners of the mats, so that they won't get in the way of the place settings.

FOOD

When you plan the menu for your Christmas party or refreshment table, approach the old favorites with a playful eye, and present the traditional holiday symbols (Christmas trees, stars, bells, sleighs, snow men, wreaths, etc.) in an untraditional medium—FOOD!

ICE CREAM

Try serving ice-cream snow men. These funny snow men will be greeted with sunny smiles, so don't be too surprised if they begin to melt.

YOU WILL NEED:
        1 ice-cream dipper (or scoop)
        3 flat round cookies
        Marshmallows
        Chocolate chips or gumdrops

HERE'S HOW: Place two balls of ice cream one on top of the other. Make the snow man's hat out of a cooky, with a marshmallow stuck on top. Chocolate chips or gumdrops pressed into the ice cream will form eyes, nose, mouth, and buttons. Big gumdrops on each side can be his arms (see illustration). Serve *immediately!*

COOKIES

Confucius says, "Life is like a cooky jar—you can't take out what you haven't put in!" Put more life in your cooky jar at Christmas.

Make cookies (for stocking stuffers, tree decorations, or general nibbling) shaped and decorated to suit the occasion and your own whims.

YOU WILL NEED:
    Pencil
    Laundry shirt cardboard
    Scissors
    Aluminum foil
    Cooky dough
    Knife

HERE'S HOW: Draw a four-inch Christmas tree, star, bell, snow man, or even your initials (in block-letter form) on the shirt cardboard. When you are pleased with the simple outline (or outlines), cut it (or them) out. Cover these cardboard forms tautly with silver-foil paper. Roll out your favorite cooky dough, and lay your homemade silver cooky molds on top of the flat dough. With a knife, carefully trace around the silver cardboard patterns. Lift out the individual dough shapes, and bake. After the holiday, wash the silver forms and put them away.

SANDWICHES

The cooky molds above can also make delightful (and appropriate) open-faced sandwiches for a Christmas buffet table.

YOU WILL NEED:
    Cardboard shapes (tree, bells, etc.) covered with silver
        foil (see Cookies,* above)
    Sharp knife
    Bread
    Cold cuts or cheese slices, or both

HERE'S HOW: Cut the bread, cold cuts, and cheese into holiday shapes, using the silver-coated cardboard forms as patterns. Then pile matching shapes one on top of another (perhaps alternating the bread, meat, and cheese in layers, to suit both your eye and your taste). This might be adapted for an Easter party, with egg shapes or simple, big-eared bunny forms. At a card party, clubs, hearts, spades, and diamond shapes would draw a winning hand.

CAKES

If you wish to turn a plain "bakeshop" chocolate cake into a Christmas special, place a ring of Marshmallow Snow Men* around the base of the cake. These snow men don't eat much, and they're so cute, you'll be glad you invited them!

YOU WILL NEED:
    A big cake with a soft icing
    Marshmallows

Clean scissors
A small pointed knife
Raisins (cut into little pieces)
Tiny gumdrops (optional)

HERE'S HOW: Build all the snow men right on the sides of the cake, pressing the flat part of each marshmallow into the soft icing. Halfway up the sides of the cake, stick a whole marshmallow into the icing, for the body. Then add another whole marshmallow, on top of the first, for the head. For each snow man, cut two additional marshmallows in half. Add two of the half marshmallows, cut side down, for the legs, and the other two half marshmallows, also cut side down, for arms. With the point of a knife, gently dig tiny holes in the "body" marshmallow for buttons, and insert the bits of raisins. Do the same on the "head" marshmallow, for the eyes and mouth (a slice of red gumdrop is fun, for a mouth). Place a ring of snow men holding hands around the cake, and you'll have a centerpiece as well as a dessert.

NO-COOK ICING

Children love to help with the preparation of party foods, and this is my favorite even-a-child-can-do-it cake frosting, because it requires no cooking at all and can be effortlessly varied.

YOU WILL NEED:
¼ teaspoon salt
2 egg whites
Egg beater (manual or electric)
¼ cup sugar
¾ cup corn syrup
1¼ teaspoons vanilla
Cake coloring, instant coffee, shredded coconut, chopped nuts, chocolate sprinkles (optional)

HERE'S HOW: Add the salt to the egg whites and beat until the mixture forms soft peaks. Gradually stir in the sugar, one tablespoonful at a time, and beat until the entire mixture is smooth and shiny. Continue to beat, and add the corn syrup, a little at a time. Beat thoroughly after each addition, until the frosting peaks. Fold in the vanilla.

The frosting may be colored with cake coloring, or flavored by adding instant coffee or sprinkling the frosted cake with shredded coconut, chopped nuts, or chocolate sprinkles. This makes enough frosting to cover the top and sides of two nine-inch layers.

PARTY GAMES

I think a good hostess should do more for her guests than just hang a few decorative doodads and satisfy their hunger pangs. I'd like to suggest a few party activities for you to try (if you're game!) at your next Christmas gathering.

Most of these games will be enjoyed by teen-agers as well as subteens and grade-schoolers. Try the Paper Party Piñata, Count the Candies, The Santa Sticker Game, Top the Tree, Musical Chair Caroling, and the Santa Story Time on almost any mixed group.

Younger children (ages three to eight) will particularly delight in the calendar-toss game in Chapter X (Big Day*) and the Snow Bells Game and Down the Hatch, following.

If your guests are shy, or if they have never met one another before, start the fun with a special Christmas icebreaker.

JIGSAW PARTNERS

YOU WILL NEED:
Colored construction paper
Scissors or pinking shears
2 open containers (boxes)

HERE'S HOW: Before the party, cut Christmas trees, stars, and bells out of colored construction paper. Then, with a jagged uneven edge, cut each paper object in half. Put one half of each item in one open container, and the other half in another open container. Mark one container "girls" and the other "boys."

As each girl comes in, she takes an object from the "girls" box. Each boy takes one from the "boys" box. When all the guests have arrived, every boy has to find the girl who has the matching half of his tree, star, or bell. Then these two are partners for the first game, or at the first dance or party table.

CINDERELLA SCRAMBLE

Each girl, as she enters, throws one of her shoes, gloves, or mittens into a pile in the center of the room. When the company has assembled, the boys scramble for the shoes (or gloves), and each boy then finds the girl to whom "his" shoe (or glove) belongs. This is a lively way to start the mixing at a subteen or teen-age holiday social.

COUNT THE CANDIES

YOU WILL NEED:
> Large glass jar filled with hard, colored Christmas candies
> Huge red bow
> Pencil and paper

HERE'S HOW: Fill a large glass jar with gaily colored Christmas candies. Count the candies as you fill the jar. Tie the bow around it and place the jar prominently in view. Next to it, put a pencil and a pad of paper. As each guest comes in, let him study the jar and try to guess how many candies there are inside. The guesses are written down, signed, and given to the hostess, who, at the end of the party, awards the entire jar to the guest whose guess came closest to the correct answer.

THE SANTA STICKER GAME

YOU WILL NEED:
> Calendar for December
> Santa Claus gummed stickers
> A blindfold for each player
> Pennies (optional)
> Crayon (optional)

HERE'S HOW: Hang a large calendar for the month of December on the wall. Give each child a Santa Claus gummed sticker. (These are always available for decorating gift packages.) Blindfold the children and let each one in turn try to stick Santa's face in or near the square for the twenty-fourth of December. A variation on this game is the calendar game Big Day,* described in Chapter X. The calendar is placed on the floor (with the twenty-fourth of December circled in crayon), and each child pitches three pennies onto the

147

calendar. The penny that lands nearest to December 24 is the winning coin.

MUSICAL-CHAIR CAROLING

Place two rows of chairs back to back. There should be one less chair than there are players. The guests march around the chairs, singing, "Deck the Halls," "Jingle Bells," or any other lively Christmas song. When the hostess calls, "Stop!" everyone stops singing and rushes for a chair. The player who does not get a chair is eliminated, and one chair is removed. The others play until only one child is left, and he is the winner.

TOP THE TREE

YOU WILL NEED:
>   Box of large gummed silver stars
>   Crayon or chalk
>   Big bag or butcher paper, or chalk (if you plan to draw
>   on a wall)
>   Cellophane tape
>   Blindfolds (1 for each player)

HERE'S HOW: If you can't find Santa Claus stickers in your neighborhood stores, purchase a box of large gummed silver stars. Then draw the outline of a tall Christmas tree on a piece of paper from a big bag, butcher paper, or, in chalk, on a washable wall. The treetop should be within fingertip reach of the smallest guest. The children are then blindfolded, and one at a time they try to paste their stars on the very top of the tree. This game is, of course, a Christmas version of the old Pin the Tail on the Donkey game, but please remember that almost everything is new to a child, and a familiar game adapted to fit a particular situation will please your young guests and make them feel very much at home.

SNOW BELLS GAME

YOU WILL NEED:
>   12 jingle bells
>   Long string or ribbon
>   Cellophane tape
>   Ping-pong balls

HERE'S HOW: Thread a dozen jingle bells on a long string or ribbon, and stretch the ribbon at waist height across an open doorway. Attach the ribbon at each end with cellophane tape. The children line up across the room and try, one at a time, to ring the bells by hitting them with the "snowballs" (Ping-pong balls). Each child gets three chances, and the one who succeeds most often gets to keep the Ping-pong balls plus, perhaps, a set of Ping-pong paddles.

SANTA STORY TIME

Storytelling is an old "Night before Christmas" tradition, and this storytelling game is an easy-does-it Christmas challenge. The host (or hostess) starts a story about Santa Claus, and each child has to pick up the plot where the previous speaker stopped and continue the story line in any direction he wishes.

DOWN THE HATCH

YOU WILL NEED:
    Crayons
    Paper plate
    Scissors
    Marshmallows or Ping-pong balls

HERE'S HOW: Feeding a hungry Santa Claus is always a good group game. Draw a colorful Santa on a paper plate, with a round open mouth. Cut out his mouth, leaving a large hole. Hang the Santa face in an open doorway. Then every member of the group gets a chance to throw a snowball (either a marshmallow or a Ping-pong ball) through Santa's mouth and down the hatch! (See Feed the Cat* for a picture of this game.)

PAPER PARTY PIÑATA

In Mexico there is no Christmas-tree tradition. Instead, above the children's heads is hung a piñata, which is a wonderfully decorated earthernware jar filled with nuts and candies. The youngsters, blindfolded, try to smash the piñata with sticks. When it breaks, the goodies are scattered all over the floor, and there is a gleeful scramble.

Why not adapt these holiday high jinks to your own surroundings?

YOU WILL NEED:
Poster paints
Large paper shopping bag with handles
Nuts, candies, and tiny favors
String
Newspaper
Cellophane tape
Blindfolds (1 for each player)

HERE'S HOW: Paint (with poster paints) bright decorations all over the outer surfaces of the bag. Hang the bag (filled with nuts, candies, and tiny favors), in the center of your party room or in a large doorway. Substitute rolled newspapers (two sheets rolled tightly, and taped) for the sticks, blindfold the youngsters, and let them try one at a time to break the homemade piñata. Start with the youngest child present, and give each child two chances.

CHAPTER VII

Fun after the Holidays

The week of a holiday finds a house filled with joy, and the week after the holiday usually finds that same house littered with leftovers—gift wrappings, greeting cards, candy, and unwanted gifts (socks, gloves, or ties that either fit no one or are fit for no one).

I always feel distressed when I have to throw away those pretty pieces of ribbon and perfectly beautiful bows that top most presents. An only slightly damaged piece of decorative wrapping paper seems to me to have some value, even if Christmas *is* 364 days away. And greeting cards are almost brand-new when they become obsolete. Here are some suggestions that will save you the frustration of throwing away all these goodies, and at the same time provide hours of fun making toys, games, presents, and other useful items out of materials that have otherwise outlived their usefulness.

A piece of gay patterned wrapping paper can be turned into a party hat in less than a minute (see Party Hats*).

Empty gift boxes can be more of a prize—from a "fun" point of view—than the gifts they originally contained. Boys and tomboys generally enjoy this idea as a creative project, as a "let's play cowboys and Indians" prop, and also as a room decoration.

DO-IT-YOURSELF TOTEM POLE

See if this doesn't make the dreariest winter day seem like Indian summer.

YOU WILL NEED:
  Empty boxes
  Paper (solid or mildly patterned gift-wrapping paper, or
     smooth brown paper from bags)
  Scissors
  Colored plastic tape (the wider, the better) and wax

paper, or construction paper and glue, paste, or rubber
cement

HERE'S HOW: Neatly wrap all the empty boxes in paper. Cut
(out of colored plastic tape or construction paper) lots of eyes,
noses, mouths, and general geometric shapes of all types—
circles, squares, skinny rectangles, triangles, etc. If you are
using plastic tape, before you cut the features, stick the strips
on wax paper, and cut through both the paper and the plastic
tape. When you are ready to assemble your totem-pole faces,
these plastic features will easily peel off the wax paper, and
will still be sufficiently sticky to adhere to the wrapping paper
on the boxes. Features made of construction paper should be
pasted, glued, or rubber-cemented on the boxes.

Work on one box at a time. Make a face; then decorate it
in as "Indian" a fashion as you can. Look in magazines for
pictures of totem poles, Indians, and Indian designs, to help
make your totem pole look authentic as well as original.

You'll have no balancing problem if you start the totem
with the largest boxes on the bottom and end with the teeny-
weeny ones at the top.

Incidentally, a family "totem" under the Christmas tree can
be quite exciting. Have each member of the family decorate
all his gifts "Indian style" and then pile the faces one on top
of another, for "opening night"!

RIBBONS

Immediately after the holidays, launder the ribbons and
bows you've received on gift packages, and iron them between
two layers of wax paper. Then wind them around the cardboard tubes from rolls of paper toweling. The tiny ribbons can
be wound onto empty thread spools. These ribbons will be
crisp, ready, and waiting when the next holiday rolls around.

CUTOUTS

Lots of greeting cards have, on the front flap, darling pictures that can be cut out. Do so! File them for the following
year. You will find that startling and original gift packages
can be created with the least expensive white or brown paper
and a single well-placed holiday cutout. Stationery and greeting cards can be made with plain white paper (or, for cards,
folded colored construction paper) and an attractive cutout.

For a professional-looking piece of stationery, place the colorful cutout in the upper left-hand corner of a sheet of paper.

SPUNKY MONKEY PUPPET

Perhaps someone in the family has just received a pair of gloves that don't fit. Lucky you! These can be turned into a pair of puppets that will be more fun than a barrelful of monkeys.

Even if you only have a single unwanted glove (quite useless without its mate) you can enjoy this "monkey business."

If you have a spare mitten (instead of a glove) you can make either Winky or Willie Talk,* two easy mitten puppets.

YOU WILL NEED:
> Tracing paper
> Scissors
> Light-colored felt or construction paper
> Soft pencil
> Any broken bits of jewelry (a single earring, a sequin, a broken strand of beads, etc.)
> Glue or rubber cement
> A woman's dark glove or a pair of gloves

HERE'S HOW: Place tracing paper over the hands, face, and tail patterns (see illustration) and trace the shapes and features. Cut out along the outlines, and transfer these shapes to the light-colored felt or construction paper. Cut out the felt or paper shapes. Draw the monkey's features on the felt or paper with soft pencil.

Onto these monkey heads and hands, attach little bits of jewelry (I sewed the drop part of a pearl drop earring to one monkey's ear, pasted a fake diamond to the ear of the second, and attached a jet-and-rhinestone button to the third). On their tiny fingers, I glued sequin "rings."

Now fasten the felt or paper face and hands to the glove. Place a dab of glue on the back of the little hand cutouts. Put the glove on your hand, and press the two felt or paper hands to the tips of your pointer and middle fingers. Dab a drop of glue on the straight—not curled—end of the monkey's tail, and press it onto the glove, right above the back of your wrist. Now put glue on the reverse side of the monkey's face and fasten it, upside down, on the back of your hand. Turn your hand over and bend your wrist, so that your fingers point

154

down; hold your pinkie and ring fingers somewhat behind your pointer and middle fingers (on which you have pasted the monkey's hands). The tail, attached near your wrist, will perk up as you bend your wrist, and if you move your pointer and middle fingers, your little monkey will walk. He'll sit on your head too. Try making two monkeys on the same hand (see illustration). Simply attach one monkey hand to each of your fingertips except your thumb and put two tails at your wrist. Then paste two monkeys' heads on the back of your hand, right above the knuckles. Now sit back, move your fingers, and just watch all the monkeyshines!

SOCK HOBBYHORSE

The sock hobbyhorse, like the glove monkey, can either be made from gift misfits (in this case, unwanted socks) or from that single sock that your laundry was kind enough to return. If you're putting the hobbyhorse together for a single afternoon of play, cut the ears and eyes out of paper and paste them onto the sock. If the hobbyhorse is to be a gift, cut the features out of leftover bits of fabric or felt and sew them in place. This little fellow will take about fifteen minutes to make, but he'll give somebody hours of pleasure, "horsin' around"!

YOU WILL NEED:
>A sock
>Clean ripped nylon stockings (for stuffing)
>A broom (either a toy broom or a household broom)
>Bits of ribbon or heavy string
>Bits of felt, fabric, or paper
>Glue, paste, rubber cement, or needle and thread

HERE'S HOW: Stuff the sock very full of discarded nylons. Insert the broom handle deep into the stuffed sock (twisting

158

and turning it to get it through the stuffing, well into the sock). Tie the sock tightly around the broom handle with a piece of string or ribbon (see illustration). Cut round eyes, the size of quarters or half dollars, depending on the size of the sock, and triangular ears, out of the felt, fabric, or paper. Glue or sew the eyes and ears in place. Tie the ribbon or string into eight to fifteen bows, and glue or sew them in a row down the back of the horse's head. That's his mane! Wrap one piece of ribbon or string around the front of his face—as if you wanted to keep his mouth shut! Glue or sew it in position. Firmly attach the center of a much longer piece of ribbon or string to the place in front of his face, where his nose would be. Allow a long loop and then tie a knot. This is your hobby-horse's reins. Hi-ho Silver, Away!

TIES TO THE APRON STRINGS

Women aren't the only ones with squirrel instincts, and a careful search of a masculine closet will uncover dozens of monstrous ties, some outdated (after all, there was a time when wide floral patterns were the vogue); others recent but unattractive. These ties can be converted into a colorful, conversation-provoking cocktail apron.

YOU WILL NEED:
  10–20 ties
  Straight pins
  Scissors
  Staple gun or needle and thread

HERE'S HOW: Place the ties slightly overlapping one another, so that they form a fan (see illustration). Pin them together in this position, and then cut at the point indicated by the curved dotted line (A to A). The center ties should be a trifle longer than the end ties. Now either staple or sew the ties (with tack stitches, here and there), so that they hold firmly in this fan shape.

Lay two other ties across the cut edges at the small top end of the fan. They should extend past the fan shape, as these two ties will be the strings of the apron (see illustration). Place the two ties so that they meet and overlap a wee bit, and pin them in place. Then sew or staple them firmly in position.

This is the perfect apron to have and use the next time the man in the house takes over the kitchen or back-yard barbecue.

LEFTOVER FOODS

Bits and pieces of chocolate, caramels, hard candies, peppermint sticks, gumdrops, and nuts can be used to add crunch and color to your desserts long after the holiday has left your house.

FANCY HOT CHOCOLATE

Drop bits of striped red and white peppermint sticks into chocolate milk and hot chocolate. The melting mint will taste delicious with the chocolate, and look lovely, swirling red and white on top of the brown liquid.

GUMDROP COOKIES

Stir teeny-weeny chopped-up bits of gumdrops into your sugar-cooky batter just before baking. The cookies will look as good as they'll taste.

CANDY SAUCE

Melt chocolates or caramels with a little milk, and you'll have a smooth sauce to pour over your ice cream and puddings.

CREAM-'N'-CRUNCH CANDY CAKE

Here's a party cake that will help, after the holiday, to use up all your leftover candies. It's made of sugar and spice and everything nice.

YOU WILL NEED:
     1 angel-food cake
     ½–1 cup crumbled, crushed candy
     1 quart vanilla ice cream
     2 cups heavy cream, beaten until stiff

HERE'S HOW: Cut an angel-food cake crosswise into three layers of equal size. Mix a half to one cup of crushed candy of any kind (even bits of bar candy can be included) with the ice cream, softened just a wee bit.

162

Place one layer of angel cake in your tube pan and cover it with half the candy-cream mixture. Then place the middle layer on top of the candy-cream combination and cover that with the rest of the mixture. Put the last layer on top, and freeze the entire cake.

An hour or two before party time, unmold the cake onto your cake platter and frost the top and sides of the cake with the whipped cream.

The topping may then be sprinkled with crushed nuts or candy. Refrigerate the cake until serving time.

This should serve about ten hungry guests.

CHAPTER VIII

Fun at Halloween

The ancient Celts believed that, at Halloween, demons roamed the earth in the form of black cats and, when caught, these cats turned into witches and flew away! They put on horrible masks to frighten away these evil spirits. A bewitching tale, isn't it? Since then, covering up with a mask has been considered the best way to face the world at Halloween.

MASKS AND COSTUMES

Here are some masks you can make that are guaranteed to frighten all the evil spirits away from your neighborhood. I don't recommend these (or *any*) masks for very little children. The one-and-a-half- to four-year-olds tend to be suspicious of any funny or fantastic face. These designs are suggested for the five- to twelve-year-olds.

INDIAN BAG MASK

YOU WILL NEED:
> A large clean paper bag
> Chalk or pencil
> Scissors
> Crayons or poster paint
> A feather, or a paper feather
> A party "blower" (optional)

HERE'S HOW: To get all the features in the right places, put the bag over the head of whoever is to wear the mask. Make two chalk marks on the part of the bag directly over the eyes. Draw a line running down the length of the nose, and place a dot in the center of the mouth. Take the bag off and cut out eyeholes, a nose flap, and a tiny round mouth opening. With

bright crayons or poster paint, color angry flashing eyes around the eyeholes, a vivid smiling—or snarling, if you prefer—mouth around the mouth opening, and typical war-paint designs all over the face. Make two slits (about one and a half inches apart) near the top of the bag and insert a feather into the top slit and out of the lower one. (A colorful paper feather will do just as well.) Draw large ears on the side of the bag, and cut along the outer rim of each ear, leaving the ears connected to the bag in the same way that *your* ears are connected to *your* head. Bend the ears forward, and then place the bag over your head.

For a surprising touch, insert through the mouth opening (and grasp between your lips) a party "blower"—one of those paper whistles that starts all rolled up, straightens out with a funny noise when you blow through it, and then snaps back when you stop blowing.

This is a good basic method for making bag masks, whether you want to be an Indian, a clown, a witch, or a roly-poly Santa Claus.

If you wish your bag-mask character to have a beard, shred the bottom of the bag in the front (where the face is to be found) and shorten the bag on the sides and in back, so that the beard part of the bag is longer than the rest of it.

If you prefer, instead of drawing the face directly on the bag, use the bag only as the base of the mask. On another piece of paper, draw, color, and cut out whatever face you wish (perhaps a round orange pumpkin?) and then paste the paper character to the front of the bag. Cut through both the paper appliqué and the bag when you make the holes for eyes, nose, and mouth.

OVERHEAD BOX MASK

YOU WILL NEED:
A box
Scissors
Poster paint
Rubber cement

Any or all of these assorted scrap materials:
Buttons
Single earrings and broken necklaces
Bits of fabric, fur, or lace
Strands of wool
Jingle bells
Ping-pong balls
Christmas-tree ornaments
Notebook-paper reinforcements
Last year's Christmas or Easter seals
Empty thread spools
Empty typewriter-ribbon spools
Balloons
Paper doilies
Paper plates
Paper cups of all sizes and shapes (including nut cups)
Cotton swabs
Pipe cleaners
Cotton
Beads
Feathers
Metallic webbing from cleansing pads

HERE'S HOW: Any large ice-cream container, soap or cereal box, round hatbox, or the bottom of a deep gift box can be used. Like the Indian Bag Mask,* the box should fit comfortably over the head, and rest on the shoulders. If you think you've got a good head on your shoulders now, wait until you see yourself in one of these.

The sides of the box (where it sits on the shoulders) can be cut so that the edges curve with the shoulders, for greater comfort.

First paint the surface of the box a basic color, and then add the features and character details. Cut holes for the eyes, nose, and mouth. Try to get special effects (for eyes, nose, ears, earrings, hat, hair, etc.) by pasting odd things to the surface of the box. Ransack the house for odds and ends, bits and pieces, this and that—*anything* that can be attached to the box mask (or to any other mask, for that matter)!

166

Experiment! Create your own monster. I'll bet your funny-faced fiend will make friends for you wherever you go.

SILLY SILKY SPOOK

Still another over-the-head mask is the sheer stocking, pulled down over the face. Use clean ripped stockings. The effect is quite grotesque and horrible, and although girls don't usually go for it (I know *I* don't!), boys of all ages adore this kind of monster disguise.

SHOE-BOX MASK

YOU WILL NEED:
   A shoe box
   Paint, construction paper, or crepe paper
   Rubber band
   Paste or rubber cement
   Assorted scrap materials

HERE'S HOW: This differs from any of the previous masks because Shoe-Box Masks do not go over the head: they are attached in front of the face. Cover the entire outside surface of the shoe box with paint, construction paper, or crepe paper. Make a hole on each side of the box, loop a rubber band through each hole, and make sure that when you place the box in front of your face, and hook the rubber bands around your ears, the mask rests comfortably. Then mark eye, nose, and mouth positions, and make holes at those points.

Now the fun begins. You can make the shoe box into any mask face you wish. For an animal, paste ears to the top of the box. For a clown, paste huge floppy ears to the sides of the box. You can even make a one-eyed monster—I imagine you can also make a three-eyed monster, but I've never seen one of *those!*

Here's what a friend of mine, a Girl Scout, did in the one-eyed-monster department. She used:

For the eye—an empty typewriter-ribbon spool, on top of a paper doily.

For a nose—a blown-up balloon.

For a mouth—a paper doily on top of which she glued half of a rubber ball, into which had been pasted a fringe of feathers.

For ears—two semicircles cut from the outer rim of a paper plate.

For earrings—corks cut in half and covered with the metallic webbing from a cleansing pad.

For hair and hat—feathers and bits of paper doilies.

PAPER-PLATE MASK

This is similar to the Shoe-Box Mask in that it fits in front of the face. The bottom of the plate—the part that usually rests on the table—is the area to be decorated. (Incidentally, the shape of a paper plate immediately suggests a pumpkin. It's not an inspired idea, but excellent if you have to make a lot of masks in a little time.)

YOU WILL NEED:
A paper plate
A rubber band
Scissors
Crayons or poster paint

HERE'S HOW: Hold the plate so that it covers the face as best it can. Place your fingers at the points on the sides of the plate that are nearest the ears. Make a tiny hole at each of these points, and loop a rubber band through each hole. Find the correct spots for eyes, nose, and mouth, and cut them out. Then draw or paint whatever funny face you wish, as in Feed the Cat,* which is drawn on a paper plate. Add any paste-on features (whiskers, hair, eyelashes, etc.), and a-haunting we will go!

WRAP-AROUND MASK

This mask project is a bit more difficult, but it is also immensely rewarding. A Girl Scout (Frances Schofield), a Brownie (Deborah Zubow), and I went to the Museum of Natural History in New York City. Dr. Harry Shapiro, the Chairman of the Department of Anthropology, showed us the museum's superb mask collection. We looked at, and tried on, dance masks from Africa, masks with moving mouths from Alaska, religious ceremonial masks from China. Then we all fell in love with a huge Hindu mask from India.

The next day, using what we had seen as inspiration, but

not as a model to be copied, we made our own. If you'd like
to work along with us.

YOU WILL NEED:
   A large sheet of oak tag (available for only pennies at
      any stationery or art-supply store), or a sheet of dis-
      carded shelving paper, or very mildly patterned wall-
      paper
   Pencils
   Scissors
   Any of the paste-on items listed for the Overhead Box
      Mask*
   Rubber cement, glue, or paste
   Discarded pieces of ribbon from gift packages (optional)
   Cellophane or adhesive tape

HERE'S HOW: The mask we liked so well had the effect of a
huge crown, so we drew on the oak tag a shape that dipped
down for the chin, and swerved up for a pointed hat. The basic
oak-tag shape also had two long panels, one on each side of
the face, to be wrapped around the head (see illustration). On
each side of the face area, we drew an ear. The entire shape
was then cut out, and the ears were cut along the curved part
only, leaving them attached to the "head" in very much the
same way that our ears are attached to our heads (see the Indian Bag Mask* for another example of this ear construction).

170

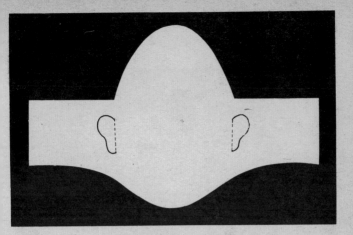

After cutting out the eyeholes and the mouth holes, the next step in the development of our mask was creating its features. We used those flat round paper butter dishes, fringed, for eyes; two feathers became eyebrows; and a nut cup was turned into a nose.

The flowered headdress was made by cutting petal shapes out of discarded bits of ribbon. The ribbon petals were then pasted together to form individual flowers, and then the flowers were pasted over the entire pointed-hat area. If we had not had lots of ribbons (we made this mask right after Christmas), we could have made a jeweled headdress instead of a flowered one. Gumdrops, jujubes, and other colorful candies,

pasted to the paper, would have given us a bright—and tasteful—effect.

When the features were all applied, we bent the ears forward, so that they would stick out, and then we turned the mask face down—very gingerly, I assure you. The two straight side panels were brought together, forming the strip of oak tag into a tube (see illustration). The tube was then taped in this position. The result was a real thrill, and we all felt that the afternoon had been well spent!

INDIAN HEADDRESS

Many road maps come folded in half, and then accordion-pleated. Leave them the way they are when you get them, and cut (as indicated in illustration). When you open the pleating, you'll have a strip of double feathers attached to a band. Don't open the map entirely—leave it folded in half. Wrap the band (with the feathers pointing up, please) around the young brave's forehead, pin it in the back with a safety pin, and let the extra feathers cascade down the back.

For a newspaper headdress, open a sheet of large (not tabloid-sized) newspaper. First fold it in half along the already existing fold. Then, in the same direction, fold it in quarters, and, once again, in eighths. Open the sheet, and following the lines you have just made, accordion-pleat the sheet of news-paper. When it is completely accordion-pleated, you'll have a long, thin strip. Cut the same pattern outline suggested above (for the road-map headdress). Don't bring the point of the feathers up to the top of the paper; let them reach about half-way up the sheet. When you open your accordion pleats, you'll have a band of paper with lots of feathers attached. Fasten this newspaper headdress in the same way that you would fasten the road-map headdress.

Corrugated paper (used to wrap appliances and to package other big, or breakable, objects for postal protection) is per-fect for making a feather headdress in a jiffy. Cut a long, two-inch-wide strip of corrugated paper—the longer, the bet-ter. Then, starting in the center, stick the bottom of the thin shaft of a feather into each little "pocket" in the corrugation of the papėr. Insert as many feathers as you have, wrap the headdress around the papoose's head, and fasten in back, and —presto!—he's an Indian chief.

ANIMAL COSTUME

Huge grocery bags and paper (*not* plastic) cleaners' bags can become funny animal costumes with human faces. Turn the big bag upside down and put it over the child's head. The more of the youngster it covers, the better the effect. Mark the spot where it covers the child's face, remove the bag, and cut out a circle, through which *just* the face will show. Then, using that circle as the face area, draw a weird and wonderful animal, reaching from the top of the bag to the very bottom. Make a huge lion's mane around the face hole, or the ears and spots of a leopard. Try making the body a combination of two animals (the neck of a giraffe, and the tiny body of a pussycat). Give your animals funny names such as Jerome Giraffe, Rory Lion, or Tom Cat. Use your imagination and you can be sure that your costume will be a success—it's in the bag!

NURSE COSTUME

The nursing profession rates highly in the "when I grow up" department. I know, because I used to do a television show with Jane Palmer, a baby nurse (she wasn't really a baby: that was her specialty). She got lots of letters from girls who wanted to know things like, "Do you enjoy being a nurse?" and, "How can I make a nurse's cap like yours?"

The first question only a registered nurse can answer. The second question has many answers. Here is the simplest method I know for making a nurse's costume.

YOU WILL NEED:
   6 paper dinner napkins
   Red plastic tape or red construction paper, or adhesive
      tape, crayoned or painted red
   Cellophane tape
   A small paper doily (optional)

HERE'S HOW: To make the cap, fold an opened napkin in half. There are now two corners on top and two on the bottom. In each hand grasp a top corner and bring them together to the center so that they meet in front. This will form the napkin into a pointed cap. Overlap these two corners just slightly, and fasten in this position with two strips of red tape or paper, placed over each other in the shape of a cross. If you prefer, this same hat can be worn backward, with an upturned brim.

To make the apron, open three of the napkins and fold each of them over and over again, until you have three separate long, thin strips. Put a few little pieces of cellophane tape on each strip, to hold the napkins in their folded positions. These will be the neck halter and apron strings.

Fold the fourth napkin in half, and (the other way) in half again, so that you have a square. This is the top of the apron. With cellophane tape, attach one of the thin strips to this square. The two ends of the strip should be attached to the two top corners of the square, so that the strip forms a loop, through which a young nurse can slip her head.

Open the fifth napkin, and place it with a point on top. Fold down the top corner in back just a bit (see illustration). To each side of this top fold, tape one of the thin strips. This is the skirt of the apron, complete with apron strings. Then tape the top of the apron (the square) to the fold at the top of the skirt. A doily, taped or pasted to the center of the skirt, will add a pretty touch. Tape or paste another red

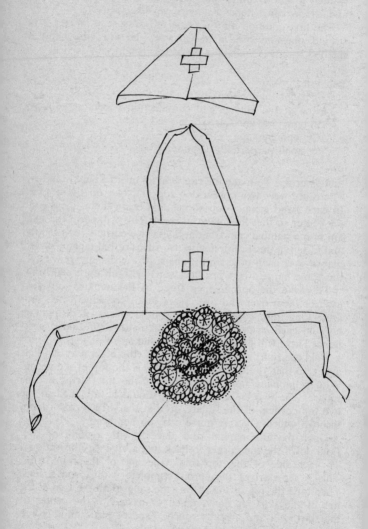

cross in the center of the top (square) part of the apron. Slip the neck halter over the head, gently tie the apron strings around the waist, and your nurse's outfit should look like the one in the illustration. For a happy nurse at Halloween, add a very smiley mask.

SWEEPING PEEPING TOM

For those children who don't like masks over their faces, make broom masks, and let them do some window shocking! Make the Sweeping Peeping Tom or create your own witch, with a built-in broomstick.

    Pencils or crayons
    A large paper bag
    Scissors
    A broom
    A rubber band or an old necktie

HERE'S HOW: Draw a horrible, horrible face on a paper bag (make it a big bag, draw big features, and don't forget big floppy ears, partly cut away from the sides of the bag and folded, so that they stick out a country mile, just as in the Indian Bag Mask*). Place your bag mask over the top of the broom, covering the broom straws, and fasten it securely with a rubber band or, even better, an old necktie.

On Halloween Eve, when "trick or treaters" come knocking on your door, extend the spooky broom mask out of the window—as if to see who's there. Nobody will be really frightened, but I'll bet they'll be surprised!

HALLOWEEN PARTY

Pumpkins, pumpkins everywhere, but you don't have to bother going through the mess of cutting more than one real pumpkin. The others can be made out of balloons, whipped soap, or paper plates.

BALLOON O'LANTERN

YOU WILL NEED:
    A round orange balloon
    Scissors
    Black plastic tape, or black construction paper and rubber
      cement
    String or box
    Crepe paper (optional)
    Thread (optional)

HERE'S HOW: Inflate the balloon and tie a knot. Decide whether the pumpkin is to be hung (from the ceiling fixture of the doorway) or to be placed in the middle of the table. If it is to be hung, make your pumpkin face with the knot

on top. If it is to be "tabled," put the knot on the bottom.

Cut two eyes, a nose, and a mouth out of plastic tape or construction paper. The shape of the features is absolutely up to you. Then stick (or rubber-cement) the features to the orange balloon.

To hang your pumpkin, tie a string to the knot on top of the balloon. To sit the pumpkin in the center of the party table, use a box of any kind as a base. Make a tiny hole in the center of the top of the box, and, holding the balloon above the box, pull the knot through the hole. Tape the knot in place inside the box.

If you wish, the pumpkin can be surrounded by a "collar" of crepe paper. Just run a row of huge basting (running) stitches down the middle of a strip of crepe paper, and then pull the thread until the strip is gathered into a ruff. Surround the balloon with the paper ruff and tape it in position.

SOAP PUMPKIN

Shape a pumpkin out of beaten Soap Snow* and when the soap has dried, paint the pumpkin orange—what else?

See illustration on next page.

PUMPKIN CENTERPIECE

For a quick and lovely party-table centerpiece, buy a big paper pumpkin and fill it to the brim with doughnuts, which are traditionally Halloween-party food.

DOUGHNUT FUN

Doughnuts can be turned into a party treat by purchasing plain doughnuts and covering them with any chocolate frosting. Before the frosting hardens, dip the doughnuts in chopped nuts, tiny chocolate sprinkles, chopped red candy berries, or shredded coconut.

The doughnuts can also help start the fun and keep it rolling.

FORTUNE DOUGHNUTS

If you don't feel up to writing fortunes yourself, you can get them from a book at your local library. Type out the fortunes on small thin pieces of paper, one for each guest, and fold them into tiny wads. Then put one into the center of each doughnut. Pile the doughnuts on a platter on the buffet, and let each guest choose his own.

Here are a couple of doughnut games that are fun for teenagers as well as grade-schoolers.

DOUGHNUTS ON A STRING

Try this for laughs. Hang doughnuts on threads from the chandelier or the top of the doorway. The contestants, with their hands behind their backs, try to eat the doughnuts. First to finish, and whistle the first two lines of "Dixie," wins. Use apples for the traditional version of this game.

DOUGHNUT SNATCH

The idea is very simple. As each girl enters the door, she is

182

given a doughnut. This doughnut has a large orange bow on it, distinguishing it as *the* doughnut. She is asked to hold it in her hand (by the bow) and carry it around with her at all times. She is warned that any boy who is able to snatch a bite of it is entitled to a dance with her. Since she must carry it with her even while dancing, other men may cut in by biting the doughnut as she dances by. Incidentally, by reversing this procedure and having the boys carry the doughnuts, and the girls on the doughnut-snatching end, even funnier results can be obtained. This also solves all wallflower problems, as the girls win dances simply by snatching bits of doughnuts! The constant excitement will keep your guests howling with laughter.

DOUGHNUT DERBY

This is a doughnut nose-pushing race. Divide the party guests into teams of two each. Then line the first team—couple—up, one on each side of a long table. Place a doughnut in front of each contestant. At the sound of the starting whistle, the players must push the doughnuts along the table with their noses. Naturally, the contestant who can keep his doughnut rolling (like a hoop) will have the best chance of winning. If the doughnut falls off the table, the contestant loses the race. The first to reach the other end of the table with the doughnut is the winner. The finalists are then pitted against each other.

SPOOK AT THE DOOR

Anything you can do to add to the spooky atmosphere will also add to the fun. For example, arrange to open the front door with a string, so that no one will be seen by your guests as they arrive.

PUMPKIN-PIE GAME

Use the Balloon O'Lantern* (above). Divide your company into two groups, and, relay-fashion, have each group carry its pumpkin on a teaspoon, from the starting line to a point across the room and then back again. No, it's not *too* easy, because every time the balloon pumpkin drops, you must pick it up and go back to the starting line. Try it yourself and see!

Feed the Cat* is a toss game using a paper plate decorated to look like a mean old cat. This would fit in very well at Halloween.

TRICK-OR-TREATING

I personally don't approve of young children going from door to door, ringing bells and begging. I know it's all in fun, but I think it's rather dangerous for the children (especially in the city), and it's certainly a nuisance to everybody else.

However, if "trick or treating" is an irrevocable tradition in your neighborhood, why not have the children beg, not for themselves, but for a charitable group—an orphanage, the Red Cross, or perhaps UNICEF, which helps children the world over?

However you spend your Halloween, I wish you "Happy Haunting!"

CHAPTER IX

Fun at Easter

The spring school holiday brings with it each year a flood of parties—Easter parties, or birthday celebrations that have been postponed until vacationtime. If successful, a party can contribute so much to the child's social outlook and grace that the occasion deserves all the help you can give it.

The party I've planned is ideal for a grade-school age group (approximately three to ten years old). At first glance, these preparations may seem adequate for the production of a TV spectacular, but actually one pre-party afternoon is all the time it will take. Everything should be done *with the children's help* before the company arrives. It's much easier if you make the party a family project.

BEFORE THE PARTY

Two weeks before the big day, invite six to ten children—any more, and you're inviting trouble! Include youngsters of approximately the same age (if you *must* have four-year-old cousins at a nine-year-old's birthday party, let the little ones stay closer to the target at gametime, and let Mother stay closer to the little ones at mealtime). Ask one other member to help you, but don't try to entertain mothers and children at the same time.

INVITATIONS

Cut egg shapes four or five inches high from shirt cardboard. Color pretty crayon designs on one side of the eggs. On the other, write the invitation details. Include time of party, address, occasion, phone number (for R.S.V.P.), and time the

children are to be home. Then cut each cardboard egg int
five or six jagged pieces, as if the egg had cracked. Insert a
the pieces of one jigsaw-puzzle egg into each envelope, an
mail one to each guest.

The decoration phase of party giving can be such fun,
would be a pity just to hang a few balloons and call it a day
It's so easy to make appropriate, decorative items out o
empty boxes, scrap paper, balloons, and other "round-the
house" materials. Why not use my examples as springboard
for *your* imagination? Working with the same basic ingred
ents, all sorts of original characters and designs can b
developed.

BUNNY BOX

YOU WILL NEED:
> A grocery carton
> Construction paper, wrapping paper, or crepe pape
>   (two colors)
> Scissors
> Paste or rubber cement
> Striped or patterned gift-wrapping paper
> Laundry shirt cardboard
> Cellophane tape
> Colored plastic tape or crayons

HERE'S HOW: Cover the top half of the box with the paper. Cover the bottom half with paper of a contrasting color. Across the middle, paste a patterned strip shaped like a vest (mine was cut from a slightly used piece of striped gift-wrapping paper). Cut long ears and arms from the shirt cardboard and tape them to the sides of the box (make sure the ears are firmly attached, for on them will hang the success of a ringtoss game, to be played during the party). Either cut "features"—including tie, buttons, and whiskers—from wide colored plastic tape, or draw them with crayons. Place the large Bunny Box at the door to greet the guests. A small one would make a darling table centerpiece.

BUNNY HAT

Decorate the guests too.

YOU WILL NEED (for each hat):
    Paper plate
    2 long balloons
    2 8-inch pieces of string or ribbon

HERE'S HOW: Make two small slits in the paper plate, one on each side, directly opposite each other. Inflate the balloons and wedge one into each slit (the knots under the plate, the long ballon "ears" rising above it). Tie a knot at the end of each string and wedge one string into each of the same two slits. This time, though, the knot goes on top, and the string extends below the plate. The plate is placed on the child's head and the string or ribbon tied under the chin. Here's a hat that will make each guest look cute as a bunny.

FOOD

HUMPTY-DUMPTY SANDWICH

Serve each youngster Humpty-Dumpty sitting on a wall, surrounded by cobblestones.

YOU WILL NEED (for each plate):
    1 peeled hard-boiled egg
    2 raisins or small pieces of green pepper
    A 3- or 4-layered sandwich

Toothpicks
Carrot rings

HERE'S HOW: Humpty is a peeled hard-boiled egg, with features of raisins and/or green pepper pushed gently into the hardened white surface. The wall is a three- or four-layered sandwich, filled with chicken salad, meat loaf—anything you wish. Cut away all crusts, then slice the sandwich in half, revealing the smooth surface of wall (a toothpick stuck half in Humpty, half in the sandwich, will hold him in place on top). The cobblestones are carrot rings surrounding the sandwich. You'll find that as far as the children are concerned, Humpty Dumpty is all he's cracked up to be.

SHINY JELL-O EGGS

Serve these in a huge bowl.

YOU WILL NEED:
  Eggs
  A needle
  Adhesive tape
  Jell-O
  Whipped cream

189

HERE'S HOW: Empty a number of eggs without breaking the outer shell, as follows: with a needle, pick a hole in each end of the shell. Then blow through one end, and the egg will come plopping out of the other. The egg itself can be set aside for breakfast the following morning. Wash the inside of the shell thoroughly through the two openings. Close up one end with a tiny square of adhesive tape. Pour warm liquid Jell-O into each egg. Seal the remaining opening with another piece of adhesive and let the Jell-O harden. Right before party time, carefully peel off the shells and place the shimmering Jell-O eggs on a platter surrounded by a collar of whipped cream.

For special sandwiches, see Sandwiches* in the Fun at Christmas chapter.

Cookies—or cake, at a birthday party—and chocolate milk will complete the party fare.

When the doorbell starts ringing, why not encourage your youngster to feel that he is the host—he is responsible for his guests' comfort and pleasure. I've seen five-year-olds rise to the occasion with pride. As the children straggle in, put a bunny hat on each, and keep the early-comers busy hollowing eggs (see instructions in Shiny Jell-O Eggs,* above) for decorating later.

When all have arrived, play the active games.

GAMES

Children love what is familiar to them and especially enjoy their favorite games adapted to the particular occasion. For example, I've had great success with this.

PIN THE TAIL ON THE BUNNY

At the top of a big piece of paper draw a small circle. Directly below, but touching the small circle, draw a larger one. On top of the small circle, draw two long bunny ears. No matter what you think the drawing looks like, your guests will see that it represents the back view of a rabbit—especially if you tell them so! Make an "X" to mark the spot where the tail should go. For cottontails, roll small wads of cotton into balls—or buy ready-made cotton balls. Put a dot of rubber

191

cement (or a square of double-faced tape) on the back of each cotton ball, blindfold the children, one by one, and stick around to see the fun!

BUNNY BOX RINGTOSS

This is another good active game, and it uses the Bunny Box* described earlier in this chapter. Cut rings out of cardboard or use rubber jar rings to toss over the ears. Each youngster gets two or three turns, with four rings to toss, each turn. Make up your own rules to suit the capacity of your guests.

GOLD-NUGGET TREASURE HUNT

A treasure hunt for gold nuggets is great for letting off excess energy. The gold nuggets are colored eggs. If you wish, they can be hollowed and then refilled with a tiny charm.

DECORATING EASTER EGGS

After the games, lead the way to the table. Then, after eating, seat the children in the play area and let them decorate the eggs. This is a wonderfully involving activity and, if they are motivated and aided with love, will keep them occupied for at least half an hour.

Hollow your eggs before you decorate them, as described and illustrated under Shiny Jell-O Eggs* earlier in this chapter. With the hen getting the better part of a dollar for a dozen, it makes good budget sense. Hollowing eggs also happens to be fun.

For decorating, collect bits of this and that—anything you can spare that can be attached to an egg:

YOU WILL NEED:
    Scraps of colored paper
    Ends of fabric, ribbon, or string
    Tiny buttons, sequins, and feathers
    Cotton
    Bits of broken jewelry
    Boxes of all shapes

Paper cups
Excelsior (from gift boxes)
Paper doilies
Crayons or ink pen
Eggcups
Colored plastic tape
Cellophane tape
Rubber cement
Scissors, blunt but adequate

HERE'S HOW: Just cut and paste (or tape) the odds and ends to the basic egg form.

Allow your guests to use their imaginations. Urge them to talk out their ideas before they execute them. This is a great help in avoiding the usual "I can't do it" attitude. You might suggest they make the following.

BUNNIES

The paper ears are attached with transparent tape.

EGGCUP CLOWN

The features and buttons are cut out of plastic tape, and clay (wedged into the small end of the cup) holds the egg in place. The hat is a cone of paper attached with rubber cement.

CIRCUS EGGHEADS

The "ring" is the top of a round oatmeal box.

→

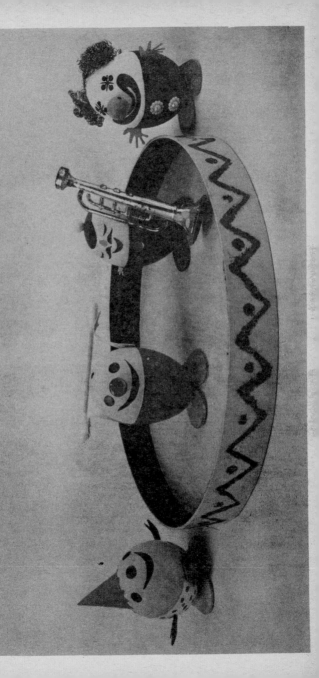

Here's a

SHARI EGG.

Let your guests' sense of humor be your guide, and Easter-egg decorating will become a party tradition to be repeated and remembered with pleasure for years and years.

PRIZES

Please plan for every child to go home with something—anything! As a rule, there are three or four game winners. As their reward, I enthusiastically recommend goldfish! They may be obtained for less than twenty-five cents apiece and have a magnetic effect on children—of *all* ages! The other children will take home their decorated eggs.

When the "going home" time indicated in the invitations arrives, have the children get their wraps.

When the last guest leaves, remove your shoes and rest assured that you've added considerably to your child's precious store of happy memories at home.

CHAPEAUGRAPHY

Whether the women in your household are over twenty-one, or mostly under twelve, you'll love Chapeaugraphy, or I'll eat my hat!

Chapeaugraphy is the art of making hats. An art, but with little skill required, its versatility is limited only by the fabric out of which the hat is made.

For the Easter parade, start with a circle of fine dark fur felt. Cut a hole in the middle of the circle. By twisting the brim, dozens of fashionable hats can be created. With the addition of simple accessories (a large flower, a pair of hatpins, a piece of jewelry, a veil or ribbon), many other lovely designs emerge.

Incidentally, this circle of felt is the ideal travel companion. A hat can be styled for almost any occasion, and what could be easier to pack!

For the very young set, chapeaugraphy is a superb basic toy. The best playthings are those that allow the child freedom to create his own fun. Clay, building blocks, and dolls, for example, adapt to the child's make-believe situation of the moment. A circle of inexpensive felt needs only a twist of the wrist to change a youngster from

AN ADMIRAL

to

A BULLFIGHTER

to a perfect little lady dressed up

"LIKE MOTHER"

Try it. You'll enjoy creating beautiful hats.

Just sit down in front of a mirror, pick up a circle of felt, and watch it go to your head!

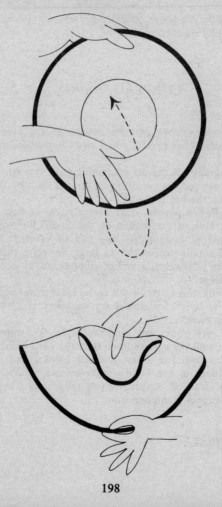

200

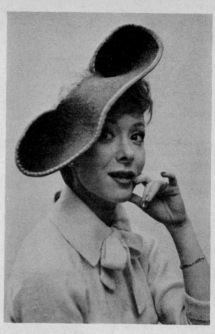

202

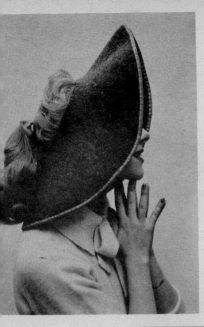

CHAPTER X

Fun at a Party

A party can be a thrilling experience to a child, to be recalled at the drop of a birthday for the rest of his life!

I remember the party Mother gave for me when I was seven. The luncheon was a dream—at each child's place at the table, a hardboiled egg was Humpty Dumpty, sitting on a half tomato chariot filled with tuna salad. The chariot wheels were carrot rings, the horses were animal crackers held together with toothpicks, and the reins were very long slivers of celery. Each Humpty Dumpty was on an individual paper plate, and as I recall, Mother had quite a time convincing my friends that this egg-citing little man was meant to be eaten!

PLANNING

A successful party can contribute a great deal besides memories to the child's bank of social attitudes and abilities. I'm afraid that, too often, Mother makes up the guest list, sends the invitations, and prepares the food and decoration by herself because "It's easier that way." Indeed, it *is* easier for experienced hands to whisk through the party planning, but then the party child is denied the opportunity to sharpen his tools—mental, social, and manual.

If possible, start planning at least two weeks before the party date, and let the child make up the party list. Then, if he chooses to invite more guests than are desirable, or omits certain children for no valid reason, the adult can gently make the necessary changes. The making (or selecting) and mailing of the invitations should be a co-operative mother-child venture.

The best parties include an age span of not more than a year or two. I know this isn't always possible, but perhaps family entertaining (baby cousins, teen-age aunts, etc.) can be done at another time.

With guiding suggestions from Mother, the theme, food, decorations, and games for the party should be prepared. Here are party pointers for three different age groups. Please don't stop at the suggestions you find here. They are only meant to stimulate your family's creativity and ingenuity.

PRESCHOOLERS

Chances are that the less you do for your two- or three-year-old's birthday party, the more successful it will be. Many mothers are inclined to overdo the preparations, even though children at this age have no idea what it's all about. Actually you'll be doing yourself and the youngsters a favor if you keep things simple. The party shouldn't last more than forty minutes to an hour, and you honestly shouldn't invite more than four guests. Ask the mothers to stay. Serve ice cream and cake right away. Use paper plates, of course, to cut down on the after-party cleanup.

Stay away from group games involving any kind of personal or team competition. These little ones just can't cope with it. They do enjoy fun, though, and dearly love things they can call their own. Any mother who provides tiny prizes, favors, or other kinds of loot for *all* of the guests is sure to be the pin-up girl of this diaper set. Simple activities, such as bubble blowing or storytelling, or easy participative games (Follow the Leader, Simple Simon, Here We Go Round the Mulberry Bush, and London Bridge) are least likely to upset any member of this group. Because preschoolers love to crayon, huge sheets of paper and jumbo crayons will keep them happy long enough for the mothers to enjoy a cup of coffee and a bite of the birthday cake.

Try to end the party at a high point. Don't be tempted to prolong it because the children are "having so much fun." They soon won't be, and neither will you!

GRADE-SCHOOLERS

For an ideal grade-school (five- to nine-year-old) party, ten to twelve children should be the maximum. Do *not* invite the mothers. Play varying games and activities, some very easy, and others a bit more challenging. In this way, everyone will be able to participate according to his own capacities. These parties generally include both boys and girls, but no boy-girl games are desirable. The hour of departure should be stated on the invitation, and if the guests are reluctant to leave when that hour arrives, inform them that the first one dressed gets the first pick of the door prizes. Then stand aside or you'll be crushed in the rush for the coats.

'TWEEN-AGERS

In the cities the subteens (or 'tween-agers) are aware of their impending maturity at eight or nine, and they proceed to become "teen-agers" at about twelve. In the smaller communities, the " 'tweeners" may not appear until the children are eleven or twelve. This age group is ready for larger parties, and should have lots of room, for its energy and enthusiasm are hard to contain. The parties may last longer (about two to two and a half hours) and may include dancing as well as games, for the boys and girls of this age group are cautiously interested in one another. (Oh, they'll moan and groan when you pair boy and girl for a game, but they'll enjoy every minute of it!)

Icebreakers and party warm-ups are excellent, and so are special party ideas. Try a picnic, beach, or back-yard party, or thematic parties, such as the Television Party* or the Valentine's Day Party.* For a small (four to six youngsters) group of eleven- to fourteen-year-olds, throw a kitchen party and let them roll up their sleeves and make their own pizza or spaghetti dinner.

Those are a few generalities of party planning; here are some specific suggestions to help you put more "art" in your party.

PARTY IDEAS AND THEMES

If the birthday party is scheduled to fall within two or three weeks of a major holiday, use the incidental material *indirectly* associated with that holiday as the basis for your party. As Christmastime approaches, a Snow Man Party might be more appropriate than an actual Christmas party—see the Fun at Christmas chapter for snow-man decorations and food favors made of soap, popcorn, marshmallows, and ice cream. An

excellent pre-Easter brouhaha would be a Humpty Dumpty Party.

VALENTINE'S DAY

These get-togethers delight 'tween-agers and teen-agers, because the boy-girl aspect of the holiday is so wonderfully blatant!

YOU WILL NEED:
    White shelving paper
    Pinking shears
    Red construction paper
    Paper doilies
    Scissors
    Red blotter paper
    White paper napkins

HERE'S HOW: The central motif of this holiday is the red heart. Cut place mats out of white shelving paper (pinking shears will give the white paper a decorative edge) and paste tiny red-construction-paper hearts and lacy paper doilies in the corners. Heart-shaped coasters (for drinking glasses) can be cut out of red blotter paper, and on each napkin, paste a tiny red-construction-paper heart.

Play Heart Hunt—which is a search for red paper hearts. This is conducted as you would an egg hunt at Easter, and the child who locates the greatest number of hearts wins.

Play Cupid—which is a target game requiring a toy bow with suction-cup-tipped arrows. On a large sheet of paper, draw three concentric hearts, one inside another. Each contestant gets three chances to hit the very heart of the hearts.

TV PARTY

"They" say that the third most time-consuming activity among Americans today is watching television (the other two are sleeping and working).

Give a Television Party. I recommend this particularly for the subteens and teens.

AUTOGRAPH BINGO

For a TV party, try this party warm-up.

If you have invited sixteen guests or less, prepare one piece of paper for each guest in the following manner. First fold each piece of paper in half (like a book) and then in half again, and unfold it. Your sheet should have four parallel creases running up and down. Now, the other way (across the existing folds), fold the paper in half and then in half again, and when you open it this time, you will have made sixteen boxes. Each box represents one guest, so if you have invited only thirteen people, put Xs through three of the boxes; if eleven guests are coming, X five of the boxes—that is, one X for each guest *fewer* than sixteen. If you are having *more* than sixteen people (but not more than twenty-five), make five folds each way, which will give you twenty-five boxes. When your television party starts, give each guest a pencil and a prepared sheet. Then instruct him to get the autograph of everyone at the party. One autograph goes in each box. This is a grand mixer, particularly if the guests don't know one another.

When all the autographs have been collected, play homemade Autograph Bingo.

HERE'S HOW: The host or hostess reads the invitation list and the players follow down their homemade bingo cards, one column at a time. They put a check in the box whenever they find that they have written the name called by the host or hostess in the correct box. For example, the host might say "Reading down, column one, box one, Jane Brown; column one, box two, Henry Jones," etc. When a guest finds that he has four checks down or four checks across, he calls, "Bingo!" And then the game continues until all the names have been called and checked. Those who have Autograph Bingo get prizes! The empty boxes (checked before the game) are free, and automatically count as checks. Incidentally, these prepared (folded) Bingo sheets can also be utilized as invitations.

HERE'S HOW: Write the invitation on the back of each blank, folded sheet and send one to each guest. Request the guests to bring the invitations with them to the party. When they arrive, play Autograph Bingo, as described above.

PIN-UPS

This is another good Television game.

HERE'S HOW: Cut out twenty photographs of television stars (from fan magazines). Make sure the star's names are not written anywhere on the pictures. Paste each of these pictures on a laundry shirt cardboard, and crayon a different number under each photograph. Then hang the cardboards around the room or along a wall. Give all the guests paper and pencil, and let them try to guess who's who. Each name should be written down, along with the identifying numbers, and the guest who succeeds in naming the greatest number of TV stars in, say, ten minutes, is the winner.

PRODUCTS

For a more sophisticated group, cut pictures from magazine advertisements and then ask your guests to try to identify the products!

AUTOGRAPH TABLECLOTH

For a lovely momento of this party, cover the party table with a plain white cloth and have each guest autograph the cloth (at his place at the table) with a wax crayon. After the party, iron the cloth between two layers of wax paper and put it away until the next party. This can be repeated each year, and this party cloth will bear happy (and permanent) witness to your wonderful birthday celebration! (By the way, after the crayoning has been ironed, the cloth can be gently washed or spot cleaned).

SCRIPT WRITING

This can be played after dinner.

HERE'S HOW: Sit in a circle, and have the host or hostess start a story. After one minute, the next player must pick up the story line and continue it. We played this hilarious game at my "sweet sixteen" party. Fortunately, my father had given me a tape recorder as a birthday present, and so we recorded the long, ludicrous story that developed, and screamed with laughter as we listened to the playback.

NAMES

Here's another bit of television fun. After the party table has been cleaned, dump the contents of a box of anagrams in the middle of the table and turn the letters face down. Each player around the table picks up a letter, and must, within thirty seconds, state the name of a television show or a TV personality starting with that letter. If he succeeds, he can keep the anagram. If not, it must be discarded. Neither a name nor a show title may be repeated, and the winner is the player who possesses the greatest number of letters when the center pile of anagrams has been completely depleted.

GAME PARTY

If your group of friends (or community club) gets together often, and you've been appointed official "party-thinker-upper," why not have a Game Party? The "games" are boxed games such as checkers, chess, monopoly, scrabble, or any other favorites. There should be a variety of games available, so that the guests can play a bit of this and a little of that.

Set up one bridge table for every four guests, or clear as much floor space as possible, for a very informal session. Keep track of the winner of each game, and at the end of the evening the grand winner (of the most games) wins—guess what?—a boxed game!

Throw a Barnyard Party, a Cowboy Party, a Circus Party, or a When-I-Grow-Up Party, but do base your entire shindig on one central idea.

DECORATIONS

Relate the decorations to the party theme. See Fun at Christmas, Fun at Halloween, and Fun at Easter for holiday suggestions.

Party-table decorations fall into two categories—the ornamental centerpieces, and the necessary candy and food containers.

For centerpieces, see the Bunny Box,* and the Teddy-Bear Box.* If you choose to use either the Bunny or Teddy-Bear Box as a centerpiece, make two faces, one on each side, so that no child seated around the table will be presented with the back of the head.

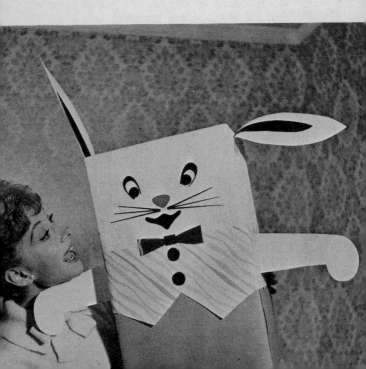

WISTFUL-CLOWN CENTERPIECE

This fellow is simple, colorful, and will amuse the children. You can make one like mine (see illustration) with odds and ends you have around the house.

YOU WILL NEED:
    A shoe box
    Pink shelving paper, crepe or construction paper
    Cellophane tape
    Colored plastic tape, or construction paper
    Red construction paper
    Ribbon bow
    Drinking straws or black paper

HERE'S HOW: Cover an empty shoe box with pink paper, fastened with cellophane tape. Features for the face are cut out of colored plastic tape or construction paper, and the stripes on his outfit are also made of plastic tape. The hat is a cone of red construction paper. Tape a ribbon bow to a drinking straw for a tassel. The fringes of hair are really drinking straws taped to the top of the box and bent so that they stick out on the sides. You could also fringe plain black paper and fasten it to the top of the box with tape (see Tee-Hee the Clown* for a similar gift-wrap design).

For a balloon centerpiece that can be adapted and designed to suit the occasion, see the Balloon O'Lantern.*

BAL-LOONIES

These look sweet and silly, sitting in the center of the buffet or party table. Simply cut features—ears, hair, mustache, beard, hat, etc.—out of construction paper. Then inflate your balloon, and rubber-cement the features onto the balloon.

Make the most ridiculous faces you can imagine, so your Bal-loonies will live up to their silly name! Now make funny bodies, to support your Bal-loonies.

YOU WILL NEED:
Scissors
Stiff paper (stationery paper, light oak tag, or the paper from a sturdy shopping bag)
Crayons
Cellophane tape
Rubber band
Balloon

HERE'S HOW: Cut the paper in the shape of a triangle, with a round bottom and a curved, not pointed, top (see illustration). Then crayon hands, buttons, tie, collar, belt, etc., onto the front of the triangle. Bend the two straight side edges back until they meet, and fasten them together with cellophane tape. The triangle is now a cone (with a hole on top), and it will stand by itself. Tie a rubber band around the knot in the balloon. Place the balloon above the hole on top of the

cone, and pull the rubber band down through that hole. To finish up this charming fellow, all you need to do is tape the rubber band to the inside of the cone and his head will remain firmly in place.

BIRTHDAY "CAKE"

YOU WILL NEED:
 Round hatbox
 Soap Snow*
 Black or colored construction paper

HERE'S HOW: If you are serving an ice-cream cake and don't want to take it out of the refrigerator before mealtime, make a grand birthday centerpiece out of an old cardboard hatbox (round, if possible) and some whipped snow (see Soap Snow* for the easy formula). Frost the hatbox with the whipped "icing," and then cut numbers—from one to twelve—out of the construction paper. Also cut two clock hands, and assemble the paper shapes on top of the "iced" cardboard cake. The numbers should be placed around the edge of the cake, and

the hands should point to the age of the birthday child.

If you want to string holiday or birthday greetings across a hall or against a wall, see Glittery Greetings* for 3-D holiday letters.

If you have recently tried to buy anything for a dime at your local dime store, you'll understand what I mean when I say that food and candy containers can be a great expense! Make lovely ones out of those unused paper picnic cups and plates you have tucked away in the corner of your kitchen cabinet.

For candy cups see Mr. I. Glass.* The crayon container will hold lots of candies, nuts, and lollipops for each party guest.

For extra-special serving dishes, see the Silly Susan.*

PRETTY PLATES

These are nice individual party platters.

YOU WILL NEED:
    Glue or rubber cement
    1 strip heavy construction paper (as long as possible, and
        about an inch wide)
    1 large paper plate
    1 *larger* paper or plastic doily

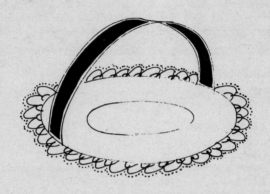

HERE'S HOW: Glue the two ends of the strip under the plate, so that the strip itself forms a handle (see illustration). Then glue the doily under the plate too, so that the frilly edge of the doily surrounds the plate. This is really a very dainty dish.

COFFEE-SCOOP CANDY CUP

Colorful candy cups can be concocted by using coffee scoops (those bright-colored, flat-bottomed, plastic measuring cups that you find in most coffee cans). Start collecting them well in advance of the party; they can be used for many play, as well as party, purposes. Tie a tiny bow on the handle of each coffee scoop, and fill with nuts and candies. That's all! Put one at each child's place around the table.

PARTY FOOD

Make the party food as substantial as possible, and not too rich—one sick child can ruin the party fun for everybody, and especially for the hostess.

Humpty Dumpty Sandwiches* and the Egg-cup Clown* will both fit in beautifully at any preschool or grade-school birthday party. See Fun at Christmas, for the shape of things to come in sandwiches and cookies. You'll also find snow men of all sorts—and flavors—in the Christmas chapter. A Cream-'n'-Crunch Candy Cake* will excite and delight birthday party guests of all ages. Adapt a plain chocolate cake to the party atmosphere by pressing animal crackers into the icing around the sides of the cake. See the Fun at Christmas chapter for a similar effect, using marshmallow snow men.

DOUGHNUT CLOWNS

In place of a cake, serve these doughnuts individually.

YOU WILL NEED:
    Sugar doughnuts
    Large red gumdrops
    Small gumdrops, cloves, raisins, or chocolate chips
    Red crescent gumdrops or licorice slivers
    White crescent gumdrops (optional)

HERE'S HOW: Place a sugar doughnut on a small paper plate. Press a big red gumdrop into the hole in the center of the doughnut. That's the nose. Two other gumdrops (or cloves, raisins, or chocolate chips) can be pressed in place for eyes. A red crescent-shaped gumdrop or a black sliver of licorice can form the mouth. Ears (one on each side of the doughnut face) can either be two small pieces of another doughnut, or two white crescent-shaped gumdrops.

SANDWICH SAILBOATS

Boys will enjoy sandwiches cut in triangles and topped with paper and toothpick sails. These sails can have the guests' names upon them, and serve as place cards as well (see Walnut Sailboat,* for sailmaking instructions—these sails are the same). Each sandwich boat might sail on a lettuce sea. Make the food as amusing and attractive as possible, and your party guests will forget their likes or dislikes and eat everything!

PRIZES, FAVORS, AND HATS

It is a bitter pill that a young child swallows when he acknowledges the fact that it is not *his* birthday being celebrated. The pain of this realization can be subdued by giving every guest the pleasure of opening one of the birthday presents (but not the same gift that he or she brought to the party). Add a bit of nonsense to this gift-opening ceremony by having each of the guests open the gift with only one hand, holding the other hand behind his back.

GIFT GAMBLE

Prepare a tiny gift for each child, and play this game.

HERE'S HOW: This is recommended only for older children who can appreciate and accept the fact that any gamble involves the possibility of losing. Have one little gift for each child— some of them very desirable, others very silly. List these in a random, haphazard way, without any predictable pattern. The gifts might include nice items, such as a turtle, a goldfish in a watertight plastic bag, a good twenty-five- or fifty-cent book, or even a ticket to the neighborhood movie house. Find (and include) other *ridiculous* objects such as a rubber spider, a plastic back scratcher, a used movie stub, an empty bottle (worth two cents for the deposit), or a picture of the host as a baby. During the party, the list is slowly read by the birthday child, and each guest gets a chance to "gamble" and say "Stop" whenever he wishes. He then receives whatever gift is *next* on the list. This can be a very comical party interlude!

These little gifts may also be used as door prizes (see Grade-Schoolers* for the ideal presentation).

EGGSHELL GARDEN

Children love miniatures of anything—cars, trucks, planes,

220

dolls, or furniture. Ingenious miniature gardens can be planted in eggshells left over from breakfast. Prepare these flowering gardens for your guests (as "take-home" party favors) and they'll find favor with everyone. Here are the directions—not in a nutshell, but in an eggshell!

YOU WILL NEED:
>   Hollowed eggs (see Shiny Jell-O Eggs* for instructions)
>   A needle
>   A bowl of garden soil
>   "Jade" plant cuttings; or Piggyback plant cuttings; or
>   Dime-store cactus plants, small size

HERE'S HOW: Hold the hollow eggshell so that it is standing on end (with the holes on top and bottom), and, with the point of a needle, enlarge the top hole. Pick away approximately the top quarter of the shell, fill it with moist soil, and then plant: either tiny cuttings from your "jade" or "piggyback" plant (these cuttings don't have to be rooted in water); or enchanting tiny cactus plants, available for pennies in the dime store. Many of these cactus plants flower, and sprout profuse red or white blossoms, each just a bit bigger than the head of a pin.

The tiny plant cuttings need a teaspoon of water daily (or at least every other day), while the cactus plants need only one or two waterings a month.

The hole in the bottom of the shell will provide drainage. Make one miniature garden for every member of the party, and place them near the door, to be given to each departing guest. Incidentally, these gardens are decorative too—see how those bits of greenery will brighten up your hallway scenery!

CLOWN-HEAD FAVORS

Table favors are always a source of joy. Make these for each child, to hold balloons which they can play with after they eat.

YOU WILL NEED (for each child):
>   2–3 balloons
>   Colored tissue paper
>   Small cardboard tube from paper tissue
>   Plastic tape or construction paper
>   Ribbon bows

HERE'S HOW: Two or three balloons should be wrapped in colored tissue paper and then placed in a small cardboard tube. Cover the entire tube with the bright-colored paper. Holding the tube horizontally, add features cut out of plastic tape or construction paper (the clown's face will be very wide). Then tape a fluffy little bow to each end of the tube.

BALLOON ANIMALS

These are inexpensive and exciting. Make one for each guest (see Balloon Santa* and Balloon Reindeer* for the easy instructions).

The Coffee-Scoop Candy Cup* is also a colorful door favor.

PARTY HATS

Wonderful party hats can be made out of balloons and paper plates (see Bunny Hat*) or out of any available paper (patterned, solid-colored, or even white or brown bag paper).

YOU WILL NEED:
    A large dinner plate
    Pencil
    Cellophane tape
    White paper sheets
    Rubber cement or glue
    Colored crepe paper or gift-wrapping paper
    Assorted ornaments: bows, bells, stamps, pictures, etc.

HERE'S HOW: Place your largest round dinner plate face down on the paper, trace it, and cut out the circle along the outline. Then cut a slit from the edge of the circle to the center. Overlap the two flaps created by the slit and you will have formed a pointed cone. A piece of tape will hold the cone in shape, and this shape is the basis for the easiest party hats. Simply "accessorize" the basic pointed hat in as many ways as possible, so that each child at the party will have a unique hat of his own.

FAN HAT

Make a small paper fan (by accordion-pleating a tiny square of paper) and tape it to the point of the hat.

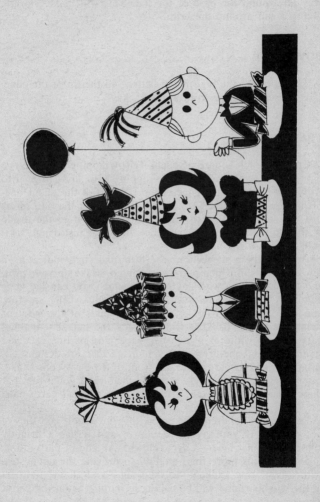

RUFFED HAT

Apply a one-inch band of paste, glue, or rubber cement around the bottom rim of the cone, on the outside. Crinkle a strip of crepe paper, pressing it into the glue in a haphazard way all around the base of the hat. This will make a pretty textured ruff around the brim.

BOW HAT

Tape a bow—the bigger, the better—to the tip of the cone. Use a discarded bow from a gift package.

FRINGE HAT

Cut a six-inch square of paper (gift-wrapping paper, crepe paper, or brown paper from a shopping bag) and fringe it to within one inch of the edge. Then tightly roll the uncut one-inch strip. Cut off the very tip of the point of the hat, insert just the rolled part of the fringe, and fasten it to the inside of the hat with a piece of tape. Let the fringe just dangle as it will, on top of the hat.

Actually these suggestions are just road signs indicating a few directions in which party hats can go. Make up your own, and decorate them with anything on which you can lay your hands. A couple of leftover Christmas jingle bells are fun, attached to bits of wool or string. The ends of the wool or string are taped, like the fringe, inside the hat. Try making hats of plain white or brown bag paper and pasting canceled stamps, animal pictures cut from magazines, or designs cut from old greeting cards onto the front of the basic cone shape. Enjoy making them, enjoy wearing them, and you'll see that there's more than one point to these cone-shaped party hats.

Remember, children love color, they love loot, and they're not critical. If you say it's a clown, and it has a brightly colored smiling face—it *is* a clown! At end-of-party time, quantity counts more than quality, so provide the youngsters with lots of tiny trinkets "to take out," and all the mothers in the neighborhood will be calling to inquire about the secret of your success!

GAMES

Add a bit of excitement to your party by introducing the element of surprise. Now this doesn't mean that you have to carry cherry bombs in your back pocket, or sneak up behind your guests and shout, "Boo!" All the ordinary birthday customs can be "juiced up" with no effort at all—just a bit of thought.

When my Aunt Lil got a piano for her son, she put it in the basement playroom and tied a lo-ong red ribbon around one leg of the piano. Then she wound the length of ribbon throughout the entire house—around chairs, under tables, upstairs and then down again—and finally she fastened the other end to the front door. My cousin was then brought home, and he followed the ribbon trail to his gift.

Here are some party game ideas that are just a little different.

"ME" DRAWINGS

YOU WILL NEED:
> Huge sheets of brown wrapping paper
> Crayons
> Red construction paper
> Cellophane tape or rubber cement

HERE'S HOW: If you've only invited four or six little visitors (to a preschool, first- or second-grade birthday celebration), give each child a huge sheet of paper (brown wrapping paper will be wonderful!) and a handful of crayons. Then show your guests how to make "Me" drawings. Each youngster places his paper on the floor—but not on a rug—and lies down on the paper. Another child then traces his outline, head to toe. When all the outlines are drawn, let each guest fill in his self-portrait by drawing hair, features, clothing, and all the little fun details—tie, buttons, belt, shoelaces, etc.

These life-sized pictures are perfect for playing "Pin the Heart on Me." Hang the finished drawings on the wall, and give each child a small red-construction-paper heart. On the back of each heart, put a bit of double-faced cellophane tape or a dab of rubber cement. One by one, blindfold the youngsters, and see who puts his heart in the right place!

[1] See illustration on next page.

HOT-ROD RACE

For an unexpected relay race, buy two tiny automobiles (with wheels that really and truly turn). Then divide your company into two groups, and, relay style, have them push their toy autos to the finish mark and then back again. The fun is in the fashion in which the cars are pushed. In this game, you win—by a nose! This nose-pushing race is like the traditional Halloween apple relay and the customary Easter egg-rolling contest. The race "track" should be at least five feet long, and any speed demon who uses his hands to steer his little car must go back and start again.

TURTLE RACE

If you want to see an amazing bit of excitement, try some of this unique game of chance.

YOU WILL NEED:
  Live dime-store turtles
  Adhesive tape
  Pencil
  15 feet of string

HERE'S HOW: Give each youngster a turtle, and put a tiny square of adhesive tape on each turtle's back. Have each child lightly write his initial in pencil on the tape on his turtle's back (the tape won't hurt the turtle, and can be removed after the race). On the living-room floor, make a large circle with a very long piece of string. Put all the turtles in the center of the circle, and watch your guests root for their own "dark horse." The first three turtles to cross the string and leave the circle are the winners.

This type of activity seems to fascinate people of all ages. On the beaches in Nassau, in the Bahamas, they draw a large circle in the sand and place crabs in the center. Bets are made, and you should see the excitement those tired businessmen can work up over the wriggling of a handful of crabs!

WINDUP-TOY RACE

Windup toys can wind up being the hit of your party. Give each guest an identical, small, inexpensive animated toy—a dancing clown, hopping rabbit, somersaulting monkey, etc. Line up your guests and have them line up their windup toys. At a signal, the toys are released, and the first three toys to cross the finish line (without assistance, of course) are the winners.

BIG DAY

YOU WILL NEED:
    1 large calendar
    Red crayon
    3 pennies per player

HERE'S HOW: A birthday is a very special day, so get a great big calendar and turn to the right month. Then circle *the* day with red crayon and place the calendar on the floor. Give each child three pennies, and three chances to pitch his pennies within (or near to) the circled date. The players should stand a few feet away from the calendar. Avoid rhubarbs by crayoning each guest's initials next to his best effort (the penny he pitches nearest to or within the red circle). In The Santa Sticker Game in the Christmas chapter there is a variation on this game which can be adapted for birthday parties as well as Christmas parties.

FEED THE CAT

The Flying Saucers Game* involves paper plates, scaled through a rounded hanger. For a startling switch on this basic game, substitute a paper plate for the hanger. Cut a rather large hole in the plate and, around the hole, draw or paint the face of a cat. (The face should be drawn on the back of the plate.) Use the hole as the cat's open mouth. Attach a piece of string to the top of the plate and hang it in the center of a doorway. Then take turns pitching Ping-pong balls through the cat's mouth. It's fun!

BOWLING BOYS

This hilarious game works best at boy-girl parties. Line up all the boys at one end of the room, and have them stand on one foot (they can keep switching from foot to foot, but there must be only one foot on the ground at all times). Each girl, standing on the other side of the room, gets a chance to roll a large ball toward these human bowling pins. As the ball rolls toward the boys, they will feel jittery (after all, standing on one leg doesn't exactly give you a sense of security). Almost invariably, with each roll of the ball, a few of the boys will either put their feet down or lose their balance. Those boys are disqualified. The one who remains standing on one leg the longest wins the game.

SHOE SCRAMBLE

A party without girls (yes, there *are* small boys who don't know what they're missing) can get a bit noisy. One good vigorous game will save a lot of wear and tear on the hostess. You can't change the fact that boys will be boisterous—so permit them to channel their high spirits into a safe scramble. Have the boys all remove their shoes and put them in the center of the room. Then scramble the shoes and thoroughly mix them up. At a signal, the boys run to the shoe pile, find their own shoes, put them on, and tie the laces into a perfect bow. The first five well-shod boys who present themselves for inspection are the winners.

WARM-UPS AND ICEBREAKERS

At young boy-girl parties the guests are likely to act as though they were determined never to associate with members of the opposite sex. They're only fooling! Help them over the uncomfortable first few minutes by starting with a party warm-up or two (or three or four, depending upon how much warming up your guests seem to require).

CROON THE TUNE

Prepare these cards—or, rather, these pairs of cards—before the party. Print the same song title on two cards, and make sure there are enough cards for all the guests. Place the cards in two piles, with one of each song in each pile. When the party starts, each girl takes a song from one group of cards, each boy from the other. Then all the guests go around the room, humming their own tunes, and looking for the other person humming the same tune.

WHO'S WHO

Prepare a card for each girl, giving her the name of some famous woman in the theater or history, and telling her to dance with a famous man in the theater or history. Do the same for the boys. One girl's card might read, "You are Helen of Troy, dance with Mickey Mouse," or, "You are Marilyn Monroe, dance with Julius Caesar." The corresponding boy's cards should read, "You are Mickey Mouse, dance with Helen of Troy," or, "You are Julius Caesar, dance with Marilyn Monroe." Each guest takes a card and then looks for his partner, who must be acting out his part.

As you plan your party, have faith in your own ideas and encourage your children's inventiveness too. I believe that creativity works like a muscle: the more you use your imagination, the more you have.

See Fun at Christmas for two Christmas-party icebreakers, Jigsaw Partners* and Cinderella Scramble,* that will fit in beautifully at birthday time.

Do you know the story about the little boy who didn't talk? He grew to be sixteen years of age without ever having spoken. but his family loved him just the same. One day as they sat around the dinner table he turned to his mother and said, "Mother dear, will you please pass the butter?" When she recovered from the initial shock, she stammered "Son, you can speak! Why haven't you ever said anything?" And the son replied, "Well, everything was all right until now."

Don't make the mistake of doing the party plotting, planning, and purchasing all by yourself. Involve the children in every aspect of the preparation and you'll establish in their minds a happy association of work and play that will stand them in good stead forever and ever.

Index

231

G

H

W

Y

KISSES
10¢